William Goddard

The Partnership

or, the History of the Rise and Progress of the Pennsylvania Chronicle

William Goddard

The Partnership
or, the History of the Rise and Progress of the Pennsylvania Chronicle

ISBN/EAN: 9783337956066

Printed in Europe, USA, Canada, Australia, Japan

Cover: Foto ©ninafisch / pixelio.de

More available books at **www.hansebooks.com**

THE

PARTNERSHIP:

OR THE

HISTORY

OF THE

RISE AND PROGRESS

OF THE

PENNSYLVANIA CHRONICLE, &c.

Wherein the Conduct of JOSEPH GALLO-
WAY, Efq; Speaker of the Honourable Houfe
of Reprefentatives of the Province of *Pennfylvania*, Mr. THOMAS WHARTON, fen.
and *their Man* BENJAMIN TOWNE, my late
Partners, with my own, is properly delineated,
and their Calumnies againft me fully refuted.

By WILLIAM GODDARD.

——" PRO ARIS ET FOCIS."

No. I.

PHILADELPHIA:

Printed by WILLIAM GODDARD, in Arch-Street, between
Front and Second Streets.

M,DCC,LXX.

INTRODUCTION.

A News-Paper becomes important and interesting to so great a number of persons, either as readers, writers, or advertisers, that the publishing one may well be considered as an employment for the execution of which the author is accountable to the Public. His skill, diligence and discretion ought to be such as to merit the public confidence, and therefore when such a person is aspersed, over and above what he owes himself, he really stands indebted to the *Public* for a vindication of his character. In this light, and under this obligation, I consider myself, and in the following sheets have endeavoured to discharge the debt, by exhibiting a full view of my behaviour, with that of my partners, and other incident things during the time I have entertained the Public in character of publisher of the *Pennsylvania Chronicle*.

It is impossible to write so as to please every body. I have little to say in favour of my performance, but this, that I have told the story as intelligibly as I could, and beg the public candour and humanity in judging of my conduct as favourably as they can; and I make no doubt but every one will make just allowances for a man touch'd in the most sensible part, deceived, provoked, distressed, disappointed, with something furnished for every violent passion to work on. I don't pretend that I am an angel, and

beg

beg only to be thought a man, though with like paffions as my neighbours. If any perfon fhould think that my narrative involves too many minute particulars, and fometimes difclofes private converfation, I reply, I have not done this, when I judged the fpirit of my narrative could be fupported without it ; but the fecret fprings and principles of our difputes are difclofed in thofe particulars, and tend fo neceffarily to give the reader a clear idea of the whole, that I fcruple if it would be poffible for him to enter into the fpirit of the caufe without them. The important fecrets of my office, are fecrets ftill, and will be fo, till I fhall be obliged to difclofe them for a further defence of myfelf—And I really love myfelf fo much better than any body elfe, that I never will lie under a vile afperfion, when I am able to vindicate myfelf, tho' at the expence of all my enemies.

The numberlefs public reflections on me, make fome fort of vindication neceffary, at this time, and I choofe to do it rather by exhibiting all the facts to open view, than by arguing in my own defence with fubtilty and art, whilft 'tis not poffible for my readers to have a full and complete view of the cafe.

The ftory is too long for the patience of my readers at one time, therefore I choofe to give it them by piece-meal, in a courfe of numbers, which will follow one another into the world in as quick a fucceffion as the Public fhall demand.

THE

THE
PARTNERSHIP:
OR THE
HISTORY
OF THE
RISE AND PROGRESS
OF THE
PENNSYLVANIA CHRONICLE, &c.

IN *June* 1766, I came, a perfect stranger, on speculation, into this city, with a view to establish a press, if the prospect should be favourable, having observed by an advertisement in the *Pennsylvania Gazette*, that the partnership between Messrs. *Franklin* and *Hall* was expired, imagining as those gentlemen had made fortunes by the printing-business, that they were about retiring from the fatigues and cares incident to it. At this time I had a very complete office in *Providence*, in the colony of *Rhode Island*, under the superintendance of Mrs. *Sarah Goddard*, my mother, and was in company with a gentleman of credit in the city of *New York*. My inducement to leave *Providence* was the earnest invitation of Messrs. *Parker* and *Holt*, who wished to see me employed on a more extensive theatre, and offered to take me into partnership with them, without removing my materials from *Providence*, or advancing a shilling; but, unfortunately, after I had been a little time in *New-York*, a dispute arose between my two friends, which gave me great pain, and made my situation disagreeable, one insisting that I should join him, in opposition to the other, unless he would submit to particular terms proposed. I laboured incessantly to prevent an open rupture, and a news-paper controversy, and happily succeeded, preserving the good-will of both. I afterwards joined one of them, by the consent of the other, till I could find a more advantageous situation, which I soon after had a prospect of in *Philadelphia*. Before I left *New-York*, a gentleman who knew my design, offered me a letter to his Excellency Governor *Franklin*, which

1

I accepted, and on my way hither delivered, and gave him an account of my business. He seemed transported with the information, and immediately gave me a letter to *Joseph Galloway*, Esq; who was represented to me as the *greatest man* in this province, by whom, on presenting it, I was received with equal joy. He acquainted me that he had long determined to have a press that would ' *faithfully serve the public*,' that all the printers of the public papers here were villains and scoundrels, entirely under the dominion of a party, who monopolized the press, greatly to the prejudice of the province, and to the injury of his character, &c. He said, he was extremely pleased that I came so opportunely, as he was about importing a parcel of printing materials, to set up an apprentice of his, in company with one *Towne*, who was then a journeyman in this city ; but having no great opinion of them, he would give me the preference, as he said I had conducted my business with reputation, and came to him with such an EXCELLENT recommendation, and would secure me the government's printing business, which, he assured me, was always at his command, whether he was a member of the house or not, and many other great and important advantages, besides cash whenever it was necessary, if I would admit him as a partner. The pompous account he gave me of his all powerful influence, and the idea I entertained of his being a man of honour, having *then* no knowledge of his *true character*, added to his flattering assurances, and the fear of an opposition if I did not consent, induced me to comply. The fatal plan was *suddenly* and *secretly* settled, and I sat out for *Rhode-Island*, from whence I shipped an elegant parcel of new printing materials, made by an inimitable founder in *England*.

In *November* 1766, I returned to this city, and found Mr. *Galloway* in high spirits, on account of his having obtained a seat in the Assembly, and the speaker's chair. Then the prospect was represented abundantly more favourable. He was then able to carry all before him. Nothing was wanting but a press " *to serve the public*,". to whole cause, he infinuated, his life and fortune were entirely devoted. He despised all sinister views, and discanted largely upon honour, virtue, *patriotism*, and benevolence. These virtues he taught me to believe he possessed in a high degree. Having thus far imposed on my credulity, he judged it a favourable opportunity to *squeeze* in his friend Mr. *Thomas Wharton*, &c. He gave him a character, if possible, superior to the one he had given of himself—In short, he was an *angelic* kind of a being, whose merits Mr. *Galloway* alone is able to describe. I am unequal to the task. Finding me pleased with the *figure* he had drawn, he *hoped* I would have no objection to admit the *amiable* Mr. *Wharton* as a partner also, especially as his *friendship* and *influence* would determine the success of my undertaking beyond the possibility of a doubt. I could make no objection to such a character. I anxiously longed to see the *worthy* original. Proper notice, no doubt, being given him, he soon appeared, and, with a certain inexpressible *dignity* of gesture, gave me a formal greeting——" Friend *Goddard*, I bid thee welcome." I confess I was a little disappointed when I beheld the *personage*—but considering that his moral sentiments might
reflect

reflect luftre on his perfon, I waited, with an awful diffidence, for a fpecimen of the divinity within him. He foon began to difplay his eloquence, and though I was again difappointed, the fanctity of his countenance, the folemnity of his difcourfe, and his primitive behaviour, concealed the man fo effectually, that I thought him at leaft an honeft upright perfon, who fcorned to do a mean thing, and one whofe goodnefs of heart would compenfate for the deficiencies of his head, for I never was fo taken in as to believe him a man of fenfe. We foon entered on bufinefs, and he confirmed all that Mr. Galloway had before told me of their refpective merits, with many additions in his way. They both declared that they only meant " to ferve the public," yet they thought it highly reafonable that I fhould let them draw fome advantage from their great intereft and influence, by which I fhould abfolutely make a fortune in a few years.—They modeftly demanded a third part of my profits each. But on my reprefenting to them that it would not be worth my attention for one third of the profits only, that they had each of them ample fortunes, and I no other way to get my living, after fome debate, wherein they expatiated on their power, ability and inclination to ferve me, they confented that I fhould have one half of the profits—for all my intereft, trouble, time and attention. Thus I purchafed the affembly's printing work, and the favour of the people, of Meffrs. Galloway and Wharton, both which they reprefented as entirely at their difpofal. Preliminaries being fettled, articles of agreement were entered into in December, *
and

---

* ARTICLES of AGREEMENT made, indented, agreed and concluded on, this firft day of December, in the year of our Lord one thoufand feven hundred and fixty-fix, between Jofeph Galloway, of the city of Philadelphia, Efquire, of the one part, Thomas Wharton, the elder, of the city aforefaid, merchant, of the fecond part, and William Goddard, late of Providence, in Rhode-Ifland, but now of the faid city, printer, of the third part, witneffeth, that for and in confideration of the feveral acts, matters and things herein aftermentioned, the faid parties do, and each of them doth, for himfelf refpectively, and for his refpective executors and adminiftrators, covenant, promife, grant and agree unto each other, his executors and adminiftrators, in manner and form following, that is to fay, That from and after the firft day of January next enfuing the date of thefe prefents, the bufinefs, art and trade of printing fhall be carried on by the faid parties in partnerfhip or company, but in the name of the faid William Goddard, and on the joint expence, charge and rifque of the faid parties, each of them paying towards the fetting up, fupporting and carrying on the faid bufinefs according to his fhare, purport and proportion herein after mentioned; that is to fay, It is hereby covenanted, agreed and concluded by the faid parties, in manner aforefaid, that the faid Jofeph Galloway fhall bear, fupport and maintain one fourth part of all the charges, expences and difburfements which fhall be neceffary to fet up, fupport and maintain the faid bufinefs during the continuance of faid partnerfhip, and fhall alfo be entitled to, and receive and take to his own proper ufe and behoof one fourth part
of

and in *January* the *Chronicle* was publiſhed, and the buſineſs in general proſecuted with the utmoſt vigour and induſtry, but with little real aid from my partners. They told me not to regard the expence, that

---

of all the neat proceeds and profits thereof, and that the ſaid Thomas Wharton, *ſhall, in like manner, bear, ſupport and maintain one fourth part of the ſaid expences and charges; and ſhall be entitled to, and receive and take one other fourth part of the neat proceeds and profits of the ſaid buſineſs to his own proper uſe and behoof as aforeſaid; and that the ſaid* William Goddard, *ſhall bear, ſupport and maintain two other fourth parts, or the reſidue of the expence and charges aforeſaid; and ſhall be entitled to, and receive and take to his own uſe and behoof two other fourth parts, or reſidue of the neat proceeds and profits of the ſaid buſineſs. And it is further covenanted and agreed by the parties aforeſaid, and every of them, that the workmanſhip and ſuperintending the workmen ſhall be committed to, and be under the management of the ſaid* William Goddard, *who hereby engages to uſe his beſt endeavours to execute the ſame, and all other matters and things under his care, in the beſt manner, for the benefit of the partnerſhip, without making any charge for his trouble, experience or knowledge. And further, it is covenanted and agreed, that an eſtimate of the printing materials, and other things neceſſary for the carrying on the ſaid buſineſs, be made by the ſaid parties, and that the coſts, charges, and expences thereof be borne and paid for by them, according to the above proportions; and that if either of the above parties ſhall fail of contributing his ſhare of the expence in purchaſing neceſſary materials for carrying on the buſineſs aforeſaid, in the beſt and moſt effectual manner, for the intereſt of the ſaid partnerſhip, that then the other parties ſhall be at liberty to ſupply ſuch failure or deficiency, by making ſuch neceſſary proviſion, at the joint expence of the company, provided the whole does not exceed the ſum of one hundred pounds, a proportionable part whereof, according to the aforeſaid proportions, ſhall be deducted out of the ſhare of the profits of ſuch deficient or delinquent party; and if either of the ſaid parties ſhall advance more than his proportion of the expence aforeſaid, he ſhall be paid the ſurplus money ſo advanced by the other parties, according to their ſaid proportions; and if not paid within three months from the time it ſhall be ſo actually advanced, he ſhall be paid lawful intereſt for the ſame until paid; and that none of the ſaid parties ſhall or will ſet up, or carry on, or be in any wiſe concerned, either by himſelf, or jointly with others, in any preſs or printing-buſineſs in the province of* Pennſylvania, *without the conſent of the other parties, except in company with the ſaid parties. And it is further covenanted and agreed by and between the parties aforeſaid, that the ſaid partnerſhip and buſineſs ſhall be carried on and continue from the firſt day of* January, *in the year of our Lord, one thouſand ſeven hundred and ſixty-ſeven* (1767) *for and during the ſpace of fifteen years, and until the ſame ſhall be complete and ended, or until the firſt day of* January, *which will be in the year of our Lord, one thouſand ſeven hundred and eighty-two* (1782); *and that upon the expiration of the ſaid term, unleſs it ſhould be further agreed to carry*

on

' *Rome* was not built in a day,' and that I muſt not expect to receive much money till the third year of the *Chronicle* was expired; that it would not anſwer for us, by any means, to demand one half of the ſubſcription money, for the *Chronicle*, at entrance, which I propoſed, as what was cuſtomary and highly neceſſary, and that I might depend on their advancing caſh whenever I wanted it, until the third year was expired, when I ſhould have a ſum due from each ſubſcriber that would be worth receiving—Yet they would, in the mean time, examine the liſt, and whoever they judged bad pay, they would point them out, that *they* might be called upon ſooner.

This ſcheme of not taking entrance money, was ſo palpably and entirely wrong, that nothing but the ſtrongeſt prepoſſeſſion in favour of the men, and the moſt unſuſpecting confidence in their integrity and friendſhip could have led me to acquieſce in it. I am really ſurpriſed at myſelf that I did ſo, and that the very propoſal had not led me to ſuſpect unfair dealing—For the proſecution of ſuch a plan had a direct tendency to diſtreſs me, throw me entirely into their power, make me wholly dependant upon them, and ſubſervient to their will. The expence of carrying on the work, without receiving the produce of it for ſo long a time, muſt inevitably have impoveriſhed me, and run me deeply in debt, at leaſt to them, and put me entirely in their power, while they might at any time have found means to

B

ſecure

---

on the partnerſhip for a longer time, all the materials, ſtock on hand, debts, and all and every other matter and thing whatſoever, together with the cuſtom and trade of the houſe and company, which ſhall belong or appertain to the ſaid partnerſhip, ſhall be valued and appraiſed by three indifferent men, mutually to be choſen by the ſaid parties, a juſt part of which valuation ſhall be paid by the party or parties who ſhall incline, or undertake to carry on ſaid buſineſs, to the other who ſhall be excluded or drop the ſame, according to his ſhare, purport and proportion before-mentioned—And further, that the ſaid parties ſhall conſult each other in every material ſtep, or tranſaction, relating to the ſaid buſineſs, and uſe their utmoſt endeavours to keep up, and maintain a perfect harmony and good underſtanding, making reaſon and juſtice the ſtandard and rule of their conduct towards each other, and that no meaſure ſhall be purſued that may have a tendency to injure or diminiſh the cuſtom of the preſs, or by any means to violate the engagements of the ſaid *William Goddard,* to keep a free preſs, according to his original propoſals and contract with the public. † *And the ſaid* William Goddard *doth farther covenant, that he will, from time to time, during the term aforeſaid, keep true and juſt accounts of all ſums of money, which he ſhall pay or expend in the buſineſs aforeſaid, and of all monies received by him, and of all his dealings and tranſactions whatſoever relating to the buſineſs and partnerſhip, in proper books, to be kept for that purpoſe, and ſettle and adjuſt his ſaid accounts, once in*

every

---

† *Theſe lines in* Roman *type, I cauſed to be inſerted after much debate, my partners wanting me to leave that matter to their honour.*

secure themselves by collecting the debts that would be due, and which they would be as well acquainted with as I was myself, and the money arising from the assembly's printing work would always be in Mr. *Galloway's* power. They could then at pleasure have made me submit to any dirty work that suited their conveniency, or any terms they should please to prescribe—or I must be abandoned and undone. —And whether they had from the very beginning a design to entangle me into such an unhappy situation, the public, from their subsequent conduct, will be left to judge.

With regard to my success in the business, this delay in receiving the money was a capital error, for every one acquainted with human nature must know, that when people are most sanguine in promoting a scheme, they are always then most ready to advance money for that purpose. Upon such occasions, when the heart is warmed, it yields without reluctance, what at another time would occasion uneasy sensations. The gentlemen, at that time, would almost have *given* a dollar each towards the encouragement of a young beginner in the business, much less would they have objected to advancing that sum at entrance, when they were to receive the value of it afterwards, and it would make little or no difference to them whether they paid then or at the end of the year, whereas it made a most material one to the printer——and as my partnership was not publicly known, there could have been no reasonable objection to advancing me the money, which it must have been supposed I stood in need of, nor was it probable I should have been able to carry on my business without it.
But

---

every year, with the said Joseph Galloway, *and* Thomas Wharton, *or their executors or administrators respectively, and, if required, pay over their just shares and proportions of the neat proceeds and profits of the said business to them. And it is further provided and agreed on by and between the parties aforesaid, that in case* Benjamin Franklin, *Esq; on his return to* Pennsylvania, *should incline to become a partner in the business aforesaid, that he shall be admitted as such, and in that case that the shares, parts, and proportions of the expence, charges and profits aforesaid, shall be as follows, to wit, Two ninths thereof shall belong to* Joseph Galloway, *two ninths thereof to* Thomas Wharton, *two ninths thereof to* Benjamin Franklin, *Esq; and three ninths thereof to* William Goddard, *who shall respectively bear their proportions of the expences aforesaid, and receive their proportions of the profits aforesaid, according to the rates last mentioned.*

In witness whereof the parties have hereunto interchangeably set their hands and seals, the day and year first above written.

Joseph Galloway, (L. S.)
Thomas Wharton, (L. S.)
William Goddard. (L. S.)

Sealed and delivered in the
presence of us,
Susannah Medcalf,
John Flin.

But through the influence of my partners, this happy opportunity was lost—and I became more and more embarrassed and distressed, as my subscribers became more and more numerous.—And thus a circumstance, which properly improved, would have given me occasion to rejoice, through this unhappy management, served only to increase my misfortune.

My partners were the cause of my printing a larger news-paper than any other printer, which led me into an extraordinary expence of near £. 200 *per annum*. It is improbable that I should have rushed into such an expensive undertaking, with my small capital, without a clear prospect of assistance. To induce me to pursue the plan laid down for me, they absolutely engaged that I should have 4 or 5000 subscribers; and I reluctantly consented, on their engaging to supply me with paper, which was a heavy article. In what manner they performed their promise in this particular, will hereafter appear.

They also insisted on my undertaking the government's printing work *immediately*, though I assured them I could not perform it with the dispatch that was requisite, for the want of proper materials, and advised its being continued at Mr. *Hall*'s, at least till I was better supplied with the particular type with which the laws and votes had been usually printed. This did not avail. Mr. *Galloway* swore by his Maker that Mr. *Hall* should never print for the Assembly while he was Speaker, Mr. *Bradford* was entirely obnoxious, and he could *never* employ him; and he objected to the giving it, for a time, to Mr. *Miller*, because, as he observed, " if I *once* give it to him, I cannot take it away, without having all the *damn'd Dutchmen* upon my back, whereby I may lose my election another year." I listened to their advice, undertook the work, and I flatter myself, notwithstanding the disadvantages I laboured under, that it was executed with due accuracy, to the satisfaction of the members in general, and with greater dispatch than could reasonably have been expected. I prosecuted the business in all its branches, with the greatest ardour and diligence, spending my own money, and contracting, with the approbation of my partners, for hands and stock. At length, the expence of the business being too heavy for my purse, upon these gentlemens plan, I applied to them for assistance, but they seemed very much averse to paying money, excepting small sums, which were of little service. They said they would engage that I should have money enough by and by. I was chagrined at this; but I flattered myself they were men of more honour than to lead me to destruction. I proceeded still, with the assistance of my friends, added to what I could raise by advertisements and other jobs, which was by no means adequate to such an extensive business. Had Messrs. *Galloway* and *Wharton* only advanced to the value of my materials, at first, and left me to pursue my business as I pleased, the event would have been prosperous and happy. They would not do this, but, now and then, when the company were in arrear, they would reluctantly advance a sum, as if it was a great favour done *me*. By such a conduct in my partners, I transacted all my business under the greatest disadvantages imaginable, and subjected myself to innumerable inconveniencies,

niencies and mortifications, by being unable to make punctual payments to thofe I dealt with.

In addition to all thefe misfortunes, while the *Chronicle* was in an
infant ftate, fuch pieces were introduced therein, as expofed me to
the refentment of thofe who are called the Proprietary Party, and
other gentlemen of reputation. Thefe pieces were in a manner forced
upon me, and I was thereby placed in the difagreeable fituation of
ftanding, as it were, a victim between two fires; for if I publifhed any
thing for a certain JUNTO, however perfonal, they would not confent that I fhould give up the author, on an application, and if I
refufed to print, I was liable to be ruined by my partners, who com-
pofed part of this *refpectable body*.—The public, undoubtedly, well
remember *Bob Squib*, *Lex Talionis*, and other writers who *diftinguifhed*
themfelves about that period. Here I could a feene unfold that
would aftonifh all *North-America*—but left it fhould be imagined that
I am actuated by a principle of revenge, in this publication, I fhall
fupprefs this and more, until I am obliged to be more explicit for the
further defence of my character, tho' the treatment I have met with,
in which every kind of hoftility has been made ufe of, that could
mangle and wound me, would fully juftify me in expofing my relent-
lefs adverfaries, that each one of them might be pointed at, with the
fcornful finger of derifion, as he walks the ftreets.—

    ☞ —— " *Hic Niger eft : hunc tu Romane caveto.*"

If Meffrs. *Galloway* and *Wharton* defire a further explanation, they
fhall have it, let the confequence be what it may; for I am perfectly acquainted with all the *tremors*, *heart-burnings*, the *cowardice*,
ineffable meannefs and *poverty of fpirit* that was fhewn at that delicate
crifis; and I have not forgot the compliments made me for my
FIRMNESS, in having faved certain ' *virgin nofes*' from *violation*.
But this I fhall referve for fome fubfequent Number of this Hiftory.

My friends in *New-England* feeing thefe virulent performances in
my paper, were much grieved, and urged me, in the ftrongeft and
moft pathetic terms, to forbear thefe publications, particularly Mrs.
Goddard, who, on the appearance of LEX TALIONIS, &c. wrote as
follows :

" MY DEAR SON,

" It is with aching heart and trembling hand I attempt to write,
but hardly able, for the great concern and anxious fears the fight of
your late *Chronicles* gave me, to find you involved deeper and deeper in
an unhappy uncomfortable fituation. In your calm hours of reflection,
you muft fee the impropriety of publifhing fuch pieces as *Lex Talionis*,
let the authors be ever fo great and dignified ; for every one who takes
delight in publicly or privately taking away any perfon's *good name*,
or ftriving to render him ridiculous, are in the gall of bitternefs, and
in the bonds of iniquity, whatever their pretences may be for it.
The authors of fuch pieces cannot be your friends, and I conjure you
to let all fuch performances be dropped from your otherwife creditable paper. My fpirit is moved within me, dreading the direful effects that have too often fprung from fuch infignificant trifling
wrangles in the beginning. Oh my fon, my only fon, " hearken to
wifdom

wifdom before it is too late—doth fhe not ſtand in the ſtreets, and
in the high places? to you O men I call, and my voice is to the ſons
of men—and alſo at the door of our hearts."—and its effects would
be righteouſneſs and peace, if not oppoſed by our ungovernable
wills. I heartily wiſh it was within the reach of my faint efforts to
convey to you what threeſcore and almoſt ten years experience has
taught me, of the meer nothingneſs of all you are diſputing about,
and the infinite importance and value of what you thereby neglect and
diſregard—a jewel of ineſtimable value —— I know corrupt nature
and our own wicked hearts will prompt us to think—muſt I then bear
ſuch injurious treatment from any perſon on earth!—Muſt I give up
myſelf to be vilified and abuſed by theſe men!——But remember,
we are not under the OLD LAW OF RETALIATION, an eye for an
eye, &c. forever bleſſed be our gracious Redeemer, who has abro-
gated it, and ſubſtituted a much more glorious one in its place, no
leſs than the law of univerſal love; and why ſhould you, or any one
elſe, try to revive what was diſannulled above ſeventeen hundred
years paſt? If ſuch writers were but poſſeſt with the ſpirit of univerſal love, inſtead of revenge and reſentment for affronts, they would
pity and pray for their fellow-ſinners, conſidering we all daily uſe
our greateſt benefactor with more ingratitude than one frail creature
can another.

"Above you will ſee a few unreſerved ſentiments of a parent extremely deſirous of your preſent and future happineſs, and however
incorrect and unconnected they appear, I yet am ſatiſfied they will
meet with a kind reception, as the deſign is to promote love to God,
and benevolence among men.

"That you may taſte the unſpeakable comforts that flow from a
life of peace and purity, and live on the glorious expectations that attend it, that the ſpirit of univerſal love may ever be the ruling paſ-
ſion of your ſoul, is the unfeigned and ardent prayer of your ever
affectionate Mother, SARAH GODDARD."

Providence, April 27, 1767.

P. S. I have much to ſay concerning our Printing Buſineſs
here; but cares and fears have ſo bewildered me, I omit it till I receive a line of conſolation from your own hand, that may, if poſſible,
revive my drooping ſpirits, overwhelmed with troubles of various
kinds, but that which ariſes on the view of your publications, on your
account, has ſwallowed up all the reſt, it makes ſuch a laſting impreſ-
ſion on the mind of your ever tender and affectionate mother,
· S. GODDARD."

The foregoing, and other letters of a ſimilar nature, gave me
very ſerious reflections, and made me wiſh to avoid, as much as poſſible, all publications of the kind above hinted at. But my connexions, under articles of agreement for fifteen years, rendered it
impoſſible for me to refuſe, without riſking immediate deſtruction.
I ſaw and felt the unhappineſs of my ſituation, and anxiouſly wiſhed
a diſſolution of my diſagreeable partnerſhip, which, if my partners
had conſented, might have been eaſily effected. But not being able
to prevail with Meſſrs. *Galloway* and *Wharton* to conſent to it, I
however

however took great pains to avoid all contentious pieces, and thereby brought upon myfelf their refentment, to gratify which they feem to have been under no reftraints from truth, juftice and humanity.—— Upon the firft intimation of their defign to devote my character and fortune a facrifice to that ambitious and vindictive fpirit, fo remarkably predominant in them, the whole pack of fmall fcribblers, or curs, that ftand ever ready obfequioufly fubmiffive to their wills, and with watchful eyes waiting to catch the crumbs that fall from their tables, were let loofe upon me, to bark at, worry, and if poffible devour me, or at leaft have the picking of my bones.

The fcribblers who ufed to pay their court to Meffis. *Galloway* and *Wharton* with libels on their *fuppofed* enemies in their hands, though in themfelves contemptible, were like many other noxious animals, troublefome and vexatious. The meannefs and mif-hievous endeavours of thefe creatures have been remarkably manifefted towards me, by diffuading ftrangers to my real character, from taking my paper, &c.

One of the pack was JACK TRAVELLER, to whom I am under particular *obligations*, for his *laudable* zeal for my deftruction, which prompted him to purchafe a debt due from me, with a view to gratify the *generous* feelings of a revengeful heart.—In order to put other unwary people, like myfelf, upon their guard againft them, I had once determined to publifh their names, but upon cool reflection, I forbear, on account of fome of their connexions, whom I efteem as worthy people, and to whom I fhould be unwilling to give pain.

My partners began very early to fhew me their great fuperiority. They frequently fent for me, in a dictatorial ftyle and manner, to their houfes, where they affumed the moft arrogant and fupercilious airs imaginable, particularly the latter, and went fo far as to attempt to examine me in an authoritative ftrain, as if I was a menial fervant, or the loweft culprit at a bar of juftice. I here want the pen of a *Macaulay*, and the pencil of a *Hogarth*, to reprefent them on one of thofe occafions, in fuch a manner as to give my readers a clear idea of them. I fhould be forry any perfon fhould gain his knowledge of them by experience. Such behaviour I believe the reader will think could not be endured by any perfon who had a grain of honour, or a fpark of fpirit in his compofition. On a particular occafion, about feven months after the firft commencement of the partnerfhip, I was impeached, and feverely cenfured, for the *great crime* of differing from them in opinion refpecting fome particular matters, and for refufing, or rather neglecting, to publifh a little piece of invective, which Mr. *Galloway* had drawn up for me to publifh under my own name, and for which he had received a fee. In confequence of this, I wrote them a letter, of which the following is an extract, *viz*,

" GENTLEMEN,

" When I was arraigned, tried, and feverely fentenced at your tribunal yefter.day, I could have offered many things againft your general as well as particular charges, had I not obferved the jaundiced eye of prejudice againft me, which induced me to forbear replying to many things that were advanced, left I might fail in due refpect towards

wards my *superiors* and my *judges*. However, though a cruel sentence has gone forth, and you have prejudged my conduct, yet may I, even now, offer a few words in my justification.

"I can with real truth declare, that I have acted with the greatest sincerity towards you on every occasion, and nothing was ever further from my intention than in the least to disturb that harmony and good understanding that ought to subsist between us. "*Arbitrary, imperious and obstinate as I am,*" as you express it, I have consulted and advised with you upon every material step, when HONOUR *did not oblige me to be silent,* and shewed so much diffidence as to carry my applications for advice on matters that to gentlemen of discernment might appear very unnecessary. It was extended to affairs of domestic economy, as well as to my profession. I had not done this, but should have acted much more without your advice and assistance, particularly in the establishment of my business, were it not for the high opinion I entertained of your honour and integrity. Though I was offered sufficient assistance to have enabled me to establish my business independant of you, yet I rather chose to give up a considerable part of my interest, in order to form, what I *imagined* to be an honourable alliance. Had I never applied to you, gentlemen, till my office was under way, I make no doubt you would have been friends to it, while you thought it was conducted on good principles; and I am persuaded that in that case, I should have had as many or more subscribers for the *Chronicle* than I now have. I am sure I should have had much fewer enemies. Our connexion at once destroyed all confidence in the gentlemen of the opposite party, whose assistance would have been considerable—and above all, I should have escaped the most mortifying circumstance that ever happened to me.

[*Here I cannot proceed without perhaps leading to the discovery of an author who has been much sought after.—The letter concluded as follows:*]

"Upon the whole, gentlemen, if you want confidence in me, and choose to break off the connexion subsisting, I shall have no objection to its being done as soon as you please, with only the allowance of what I brought with me, and what it shall appear I am justly entitled to.

I am, respectfully, Gentlemen,
Your humble servant,
WILLIAM GODDARD."

July 22, 1 67.

Messrs. *Joseph Galloway*, and
    Thomas Wharton.

On the receipt of the above, I was sent for to Mr. *Galloway's* house, where both he and Mr. *Wharton* used all the art and sophistry they were masters of, to smooth over their late proceedings, and finally made me such solemn promises to support me in a very extraordinary manner, by performing a former engagement, of advancing me £.500 sterling each, to establish me in a book store, that I was dissuaded

suaded from my thoughts of a separation. I went on in business for
some time with great satisfaction, and with very considerable success,
and my partners behaved with a becoming moderation, which gave
me hopes that I should enjoy the blessings of freedom, and that they
would in future treat me as a partner ought to be treated. But alas!
my pleasing ideas were ere long dispelled. My partners being of
such an unhappy make, that *when they can no longer plague other people,
they become a plague to themselves,* could not be quiet but a little
time. They saw a new cause of complaint against me. The *Farmer's* Letters appeared in the *Chronicle, supposed* to be written by the
ingenious Mr. *Dickinson,* a gentleman, whom, at that time, I had never seen. Here the ignorance of Mr. *Wharton,* and the envy of Mr.
Galloway, and the wickedness of both united were clearly manifested.
They were angry, they fretted, they *swore* and *affirmed,* that they
were too inflammatory for this latitude. While Mr. *Galloway* ex-
claimed, with a countenance expressive of the deepest envy, that they
were " *damned ridiculous! meer stuff! fustian! altogether stupid and
inconsistent!—only a compilation by* Dickinson *and* Thomson!" the very
sagacious and *deep-read* Mr. *Wharton,* with a great deal of solemn
dump and grimace in his look, signified that " Friend *Goddard* was
very *imprudent* in introducing such pieces into our *Chronicle,* at such a
time—that he observed, with no small concern, that I published
pieces that were inconsistent with *their* views in establishing a press,
and that I should not go on head-long against the interest of my BE-
NEFACTORS." I *presumed* to reason with them, and assured them that
the letters were extremely agreeable to the people, and for my part, I
thought they deserved the serious attention of all *North-America.* Mr.
Galloway ridiculed my notions about liberty and the rights of mankind, and observed that ' the people in *America* were mad—they knew
not what they wanted—and indeed were incapable of judging on
such matters—that such factious pieces would answer for the select-
men of *Boston,* and the mob meetings of *Rhode-Island,* but he was
sure they would soon be despised here, *Pennsylvanians* (a few hot-
headed people excepted) being of a different make, of more solidity,
none of *your* damned republican breed—but loyal to the king, and
friends to monarchy—that they had great expectations from the favour of the ministry, and that such performances would injure the
province at the *British* court, and shew that they were as refractory as
the other colonies, and that they might thereby destroy their *best
hopes centered in their agent.*' I formed my own opinions of the men,
waved conversing upon such subjects, and still continued, with my
usual " *obstinacy,*" as they expressed themselves, to publish the letters,
and every other patriotic piece which I judged had the least tendency
to promote the common cause of this much injured country. The
Farmer's Letters grew more and more admired, and these *gentlemen*
then judged it dangerous *openly* to declaim against them, or vilify
their supposed author. They therefore would call together a select
number of malecontents, to whom they would disgorge their malig-
nity of heart, and who would, without remorse, circulate their calumnies abroad. I could here call forth a series of letters dated *Virginia,*

ginia, but wrote in *Philadelphia*, now depofited in a certain deſk, de-
ſigned for a complete anſwer to the *Farmer's* letters ; but I ſuppreſs
this at preſent, tho' the *worthy* author once ſaid to a gentleman of my
acquaintance, on a little difagreement—" *Take care what you fay and
do, Sir—You have unboſomed yourſelf to me—I know the fecrets of your
heart—you have made me your boſom friend.*"

The celebrated Dean *Swift* obſerves, that ' a man ſhould never be
aſhamed to own he has been in the wrong, which is but ſaying, in
other words, he is wiſer to-day, than he was yeſterday.' I heartily
join with him—and muſt frankly acknowledge, that I went too great
lengths to gratify theſe men—But when my ſituation is confidered,
that I was young and unexperienced, that I was impoſed upon by their
artifices, or awed by an idea of their power, &c. I flatter myſelf I
ſhall, as to honeſty, redeem my character, tho' it ſhould be at ' the
expence of that of my underſtanding,'—eſpecially as I can declare,
with the utmoſt truth, that I entertained no prejudices againſt any
perſons whatſoever in this province, and came here with a view to
promote my intereſt by an honourable proſecution of my buſineſs,
without becoming a party in any difputes—and had I been ſo happy
as to have eſcaped the ſnares of Meſſrs. *Galloway* and *Wharton*, I per-
ſuade myſelf I ſhould not now ſtand in need of an apology.

I am perfectly convinced that the *firſt* magiſtrates of this province,
Mr. *Hicks*, Mr. *Dickinſon*, Mr. *Thomſon*, and ſeveral other gentlemen, have been very injuriouſly treated in the *Chronicle* ; and as far
as I ſhall have opportunity, I will do juſtice to their characters, and
make them all the *retaliation* in my power ; and my future conduct in
life ſhall ſhew them, and the public, that my principles lead me to
do juſtice to all mankind. I ever acted in the moſt impartial and
juſt manner, as a printer, when I was ſuffered, by my overbearing
partners, to follow my own inclination, and enjoy the leaſt freedom
of action—And my ardent deſire is, that the diſgrace and ſcandal
may be removed from my door, and be placed where it is juſtly me-
rited. I have borne it too long. I cannot but flatter myſelf that even
the gentlemen who have been ſo notoriouſly abuſed, will be ſo candid as to make the proper allowances, and not impute to me what
is the crime of others.

It gave me the moſt painful ſenſations to find myſelf deeply connected with men who were enemies to their country, and as ſuch obnoxious to many worthy characters who wiſhed to be my friends; and
I deplored that I had been ſo miſled as to form ſuch an unnatural alliance, as I thereby loſt the good-will of thoſe whom, of all mankind, I reſpected, and whoſe friendſhip I ſhould have cultivated. I
received ſome hints of my danger, but they were communicated
either at times when I had the greateſt confidence in my partners,
or when I was ſo entangled with them, as to render a ſeparation
extremely hazardous. One gentleman of great worth and abilities,
in an adjacent province, wrote me as follows, *viz.*

" DEAR SIR,

" It gave me no ſmall pleaſure, that amidſt the variety of objects,
which in your ſituation muſt demand your attention, you ſhould ne-

C   vertheleſs,

vertheless pleafe to teftify the place I have in your mind, by writing
me a letter. I thank you, and rejoice at your profpect of fuccefs in
your bufinefs.

"I think, Sir, that your determination of devoting your paper to
the general and true intereft of *America*, as well as to the particular
advantage of your colony, is well chofen—but I am exceedingly fearful that your connexions will cramp you in your noble views. I
hear, with regret, that you have admitted two men as partners with
you, who have been notorious enemies of their country, and one of
them the infamous *Americanus*, whofe performances I fend you in-
clofed, with fome remarks[*]—Take care, my friend, how you truft
thefe men. Thofe who would betray their country, cannot be depended on as friends in a day of trial. I hope you have acted with
proper caution in your agreement with them, and that the iffue will
terminate to your honour and intereft. I admire the plan of the
Chronicle; and if the true intereft of all the *North-American* colonies
in general is confidered therein, and fuch meafures and attempts for
enflaving a great and free people, as have been and may be entered
into or made, be fuitably and with due fervour expofed, the merit of
your *Chronicle* will rife in proportion to the extenfion of fuch important fubjects.

"See that the fpirit of your paper be kept up; for if the fire fhould
ceafe, it will be no more than a common news-paper, and will be as
little attended to as any other trite and common thing. Fear not, and
you fhall do well. Your friend and humble fervant, ******."

The *Farmer's* Letters having been publifhed with univerfal ap-
plaufe, throughout the continent, the worthy author began to receive
the generous acknowledgments of his grateful countrymen. Thefe
were very offenfive to my partners, who were apprehenfive that the
inhabitants of this city and county would, at the next election, give
him their fuffrages as a reprefentative, and make him a guardian of
thofe rights, which he had fo ably and fo zealoufly defended, in
which cafe they imagined he would, as he had done before, "*mar*
all their plans." A fignal from them was fufficient to raife up a hoft
of angry fcribblers, who were ever ready to draw their fervile pens, in
the moft of caufes, againft the beft. It became at length a very
ferious matter with a certain cabal, and the word went forth——"*No*
Farmer in the affembly."——There then were crouded upon me a
number . . . againft the *Farmer*, &c. under the fignatures of *A
Countryman*, *A Miller*, *Frank Meanwell*, *Jack White Oak*, *A Bar-
badian*, *A Country Farmer*, *Son of Liberty*, &c. &c. I found myfelf
obliged to publifh them, tho' I was very averfe to it, and was confident it would terminate in the lofs of many good cuftomers, which
was really the cafe. Thefe publications gave my partners much
pleafure; they complimented me, declared that I was "now in
the right way," that they would make my fortune, if I would but
attend to the advice of my *real* friends, meaning themfelves, and gave
out every where that I printed the beft paper in the King's dominions.
But all this could not compenfate for the uneafinefs I gave my
friends,

---

[*] *Thefe pieces will be publifhed in the next number.*

friends,* and the concern I felt in being reduced to fuch a cruel alter-
native—either to abufe a man I highly efteemed, or fall an immediate
facrifice to party fury and refentment ——My friends in *New-Eng-*
land, and a number of gentlemen in this province, on the firft appearance of the *Farmer's* Letters, engaged to take feveral hundred
of them, in cafe I would reprint them in a handfome pamphlet.† I
mentioned this to my partners; but they objected to my doing it in
fuch a manner as difcouraged me—fo that their ill will to the author,
and their enmity to liberty and the good of mai kind, deprived me of
a job that would have produced a handfome fum, which fell into
other hands.

Some time in *May* 1768, my partners gave me an invitation to
fpend an evening with them. I waited on them accordingly; and
after they had treated me with much complaifance, they told me
they had heard a great character of my mother; and as I was a
young man, in a very valuable and extenfive bufinefs, they confidered it too laborious a tafk for me to manage every department, *i. e.*
to fuperintend the workmen in the Printing-Office, keep the accounts, collect and digeft the news and manufcripts, difpatch the
news-papers, write the neceffary letters, and attend to providing for
a large family, they therefore propofed to me to difpofe of my bufinefs at *Providence*, put my money into ftock, and bring my family
here, promifing to take a genteel houfe for us, and not only to al-
low my mother a reafonable fum for her fuperintendance of family
affairs, but to advance a fum fufficient to eftablifh her in a ftore of
books and ftationary. I made many objections, telling them that I
might not fucceed here agreeable to my hopes, and that I chofe to
have a place to which I could retire, and be well received; befides,
in fuch cafe, I muft refign my commiffion in the Poft-Office, which
was of fome advantage to my family. They laughed at my fears
and unwillingnefs, and expreffed fo much aftonifhment at my hefi-
tating

Extract of a letter from Mrs. Goddard, *of* Providence, *to* W.
Goddard, *in* Philadelphia.

" *It is no fmall concern to me, and all who wifh you well, to fee fo*
many abufive pieces inferted in the Chronicle *againft the* Farmer, *who*
deferves fo well of his country. Do not, I befeech you, fully all the ho-
nour you have acquired by uniting with the enemies of your country,
againft the beft men in it. The keeping up difputes in your paper in a
bitter way, is no ways agreeable to the temper and genius of a chriftian,
and your banifhing them out of the limits of your paper, would, in the
higheft manner, gratify me. Don't be purfuing fhadows, but feek dura-
ble riches, and every neceffary thing will be added, for all earthly en-
joyments can never fatisfy an immortal foul, but leaves it poor and blind
and naked. I cannot forbear fpeaking firft of fuch a momentous truth,
but from things of infinite importance, I fly to thofe of lefs regard."——
† *Extract of a letter from Mrs.* Goddard, *at* Providence, *to* W.
Goddard, *in* Philadelphia.

" *Your friend Judge* C—e, *and I think it would be a good fcheme*
in you to print the Farmer's *Letters in a pamphlet, and that foon, as*
they appear to be the completeft pieces ever wrote on the fubject in America. *They are univerfally admired here.*"

tating to accept of such *disinterested generous* offers, that I gave way to
their solicitations, and accordingly wrote a letter to my mother on
the subject—to which she made this reply :—" I observe what you say
" about Messrs. *Galloway* and *Wharton*'s advising you to endeavour to
" prevail on me to leave *Providence* ; but as I have entered with peo-
" ple for a year's news, I choose to continue here till it is concluded,
" and always if I can ; for my life is almost at a close, and I can
" hardly think of removing so near the period of my days into a
" strange part of the world, to launch into a new set of acquaint-
" ance, and leave all my former ones, the companions of my
" youth, and the supporters of my old age, as well as my daughter,
" who seems by nature designed to take care of her mother in sick-
" ness, when wanted, which is not so properly the sphere of sons,
" and cannot be expected of them." Upon shewing this to my partners, they prevailed upon me to visit her in person. This I did, and
laid the prospect before her, and she, from motives of maternal ten-
derness, consented to leave an easy agreeable situation, and a multi-
tude of amiable friends, and my sister agreed to accompany her. In
consequence of this, I gave up the Post-Office, and disposed of my
Printing-Office for 550 dollars to a young man, of this city, who I
had established in business as a partner with my mother, payable the
December next following. This business being finished, I left my
family to prepare for their departure, and returned to *Philadelphia*
with all expedition.

About this time two pieces were offered for publication, which
were highly derogatory to the honour of a clergyman, and another
gentleman of reputation, and calculated to stir up strife and animo-
sity between the inhabitants of *Pennsylvania* and the *New-England*
provinces, which I thought would have a very bad tendency at a time
when our liberties were in imminent danger, and their preservation
depended on our union with one another. These I refused to publish,
unless I was allowed to disclose the authors names, on an application from the person who should suppose himself injured, or be permitted to omit the exceptionable passages. Neither of my proposals
were agreed to, but the authors took away their manuscripts in a great
rage, declaring that they would paint me in my " *native colours*"—
that I was " *an enemy to the church, and a friend to the kirks and yellow
wigs*"—that I had frequently ' *presumed*' to propose alterations in their
performances, but they were determined no longer to *submit* to ME in
such matters. I have part of this signed with their own names, in their
own hand writing. As *I* was no longer to be *submitted* to, a heavy
complaint was made against me to my two partners. I was called to
account, very critically examined, and finally, after I had made use
of every argument in my power, I was found guilty of *not* publishing what I ought to have published, and condemned, without mer-
cy, both Messieurs *Galloway* and *Wharton* declaring that I had no
right to interfere in such a way; but as I had engaged to keep
a *free* and *secret* press, I should have published those pieces (which
I do assure my readers would have made me infamous in the eyes
of every honest man) without pretending to altercate with men
who were so capable of injuring my business, and who were *their*

warm friends. We could not agree in fentiment. Mr. *Wharton* was *infolent* beyond expreffion, and as *ftupid* as he was *infolent.* The GENTLE *Galloway* too, in his own houfe, could act the tyrant—he could there ftorm and rave and fwear—" By G—d, Sir, you mean " to knock up the prefs—Don't think WE are to be ruled by YOU, " or that we cannot have a prefs that will ferve us," *i. e.* the public. " You are not in *Rhode-Ifland* now—You have too much of the " damn'd *New-England* fpirit—You kept *New-York* in a flame in " oppofition to the ftamp-act"—and added, that fuch a conduct would not do in *Pennfylvania,* that they were a fober folid people—that I was a *Prefbyterian* he was fure, &c. &c.

Vexed at fuch treatment I could not help retorting with fome acrimony. I told them that their charges againft me were very illiberal, and fcarcely deferved an anfwer—that I was ready to ferve them and their friends as far as my confcience would permit me—that my conduct at *New-York* would have done honour to thofe who cenfured me : and as to the charge of my being a *Prefbyterian,* I told them I had nothing to fay—that I did not imagine when they entered into partnerfhip with me, that they would interfere with my confeffion of faith. To this Mr. *Wharton* replied, —" Whatever *thee* may think, *William Geddard,* if fuch an opinion fhould obtain here, that *thee* art a *Prefbyterian,* it would not be to thy intereft, think of it as *thee will."* I could not help fmiling on the occafion, but it was a fmile of the greateft contempt, and I ufed fome expreffion which touched Mr. *Galloway* fo fenfibly, that he began very *heroically* to *ftamp* on his own floor, faying with an emphafis, that I muft ufe no more *farcafm* with them, that I was very apt to deal forth fuch *ftrokes* as were not agreeable, &c. To avoid farther infult, I haftily left them, with aftonifhment and indignation.—Upon their confidering their behaviour, and how little they were like to gain by it, they became more *calm* and *civilized,* and endeavoured to make me believe that what had paffed at the laft meeting, arofe from a *warm zeal* for the intereft of my bufinefs, and that fudden fallies of paffion fhould not be regarded, or be confidered a breach of friendfhip. Their behaviour was feemingly fo very *friendly* and *kind,* that I became willing to forget the ill treatment I had met with.

In *November* 1768, my mother and fifter arrived. I immediately acquainted my partners with it, expecting a performance of their promifes ; but I was difappointed—for inftead of paying fome attention to an ancient gentlewoman, whofe removal they had occafioned, they treated her with a total neglect. I felt moft fenfibly on the occafion, yet I endeavoured to conceal my anxiety from my friends. Finding fuch perfidy and inhumanity in my partners, I took a houfe and removed into it, and while myfelf and family were all induftrioufly employed in regulating our affairs, upon the ftricteft plan of economy, and profecuting the bufinefs with the greateft care and attention, Mr. *Wharton,* to my furprife, appeared, and accofted me in a very abrupt manner, whereupon a dialogue arofe between us, which, in juftice to Mr. *Wharton,* I cannot avoid inferting—and I hope my repeating it exactly in the ftyle in which it was expreffed, will not by any be conftrued into a defign to ridicule that, or the denomination of *Chriſtians* by whom it is uſed (without Mr. *Wharton's* barbariſms) and for wt om I entertain ſentiments of very high reſpect.

DIALOGUE.

Wharton. *William Goddard*, we do not approve of thy proceedings.

Goddard. Why Mr. *Wharton?*

Wharton. *Thee has* taken a houſe very unſuitable to thee. How came thee to do it, without firſt conſulting *Joſeph Galloway* and myſelf?

Goddard. It is a very convenient houſe, Sir, and a good neighbourhood. I like it very much Sir.

Wharton. That is not what I mean—I tell thee *William*, we diſapprove of thy proceedings.

Goddard. This Mr. *Wharton* you might have prevented, by an attention to your *ſolemn* promiſe.

Wharton. I tell thee Friend *Goddard*, *thee has* done wrong—and *thee ſhall* ſuffer for it. A houſe in an alley would anſwer thy purpoſe well enough.

Goddard. Mr. *Wharton*, if you have no reſpect for my friends, I will ſhew them that I have; and as we did not come out of an *alley*, we will not be driven into one by Mr. *Wharton.*

Wharton. Very well, young man! *thee ſhall* ſmart for this.

He retires, comes again, and renews the dialogue.

Wharton. I have ſomething more to ſay to thee.

Goddard. Very well, Mr. *Wharton*, I ſhall attend to you.

Wharton. Friend *Goddard*, I have been told *thee has* removed a preſs into thy mother's houſe, which is a proceeding I very much diſlike.

Goddard. I did this to oblige my mother, Sir, who requeſted me to let her have a preſs for the printing blanks and ſmall work, while I conducted the large.

Wharton. *William Goddard*, *thee has* ſiniſter views.

Goddard. Mr. *Wharton* I have no views but ſuch as are upright, and my intention, and that of my friends, is only to ſerve the company.

Wharton. I am confident *thee intends* to ſet up a preſs *independent* of us—therefore, without multiplying words, I order thee *William Goddard*, to bring that preſs immediately back. *Thee ſhall* do it, or we'll take meaſures that ſhall be unwelcome to thee.

Goddard. I ſhall adviſe with my mother, and if it is her mind that I comply with your requeſt, I will gratify you—and on no other terms.

Wharton. See that *thee* do'ſt it.

I was a little diverted, while I deſpiſed the arrogance of this reſtleſs man, his gigantic ſtrides, and oſtentatious ſwelling. Upon relating the matter to my mother, we had much laugh, at the expence of *poor* Mr. *Wharton*, yet ſhe recommended my returning the materials, rather than have any diſpute with ſuch a " *diſſatisfied genius.*" This I complied with; but the moſt condeſcending and ſubmiſſive behaviour would not ſatisfy my partners, but paved the way for further ſpecimens of their ſovereignty ever me. Nothing would pleaſe

them,

them, but an entire fubmiffion to their will and pleafure, and a total
furrender of my honour and intereft *at difcretion.* I was ftill a "*refractory New-Englandman*," and could not be made a venal party tool,
nor fuffer myfelf to be moulded into what fhape they pleafed. Yet, as I
was fo linked in with them as to be unable to extricate myfelf, I judged it prudent to cultivate their friendfhip, for my prefervation, until
the happy time fhould arrive, when I could be delivered from the
thraldom I was in—provided I could do it, and not violate my honour. By a guarded conduct, affairs went on very well a while; but it
was impoffible for Mr. *Wharton* to let any man with whom he had a
connexion enjoy a tranquil life. He foon worked up Mr. *Galloway* into a belief that I was an enemy to their *great plan* of effecting
a change in the conftitution of this province, and a *fecret* friend to
their enemies, &c. They therefore went fo far, in direct oppofition to
our agreement, as to propofe and *infift* upon my taking in a *reprefentative* of themfelves into the printing-office, whereby they might
always have a fight of my manufcripts, over-rule me in my publications, fupprefs truth and juftice, and completely enflave me and my
prefs, to the ruin of my character as a man of integrity. Mr. *Towne,*
my journeyman, and their *private intelligencer,* was to be the *reprefentative* of this *patriotic* duumvirate, whofe views were *only* " to
ferve the public." This extraordinary *demand* occafioned a frefh dialogue between *friend Wharton* and me.

More D I A L O G U E, Gentlemen and Ladies!

Wharton. Friend *Goddard,* we have advanced, from time to time,
very confiderable fums to eftablifh a prefs—We have great intereft in
thy prefs—We are determined to have a prefs that will *ferve the
public*——We think we are not properly *reprefented* in thy office.
Thee does as *thee pleafes*—*Thee* feldom comes near *Jofeph Galloway*
and myfelf—*Thee keeps* company with people of the wrong fide of
the queftion—I have to no purpofe cautioned thee againft fuch a
conduct. *Thee knows* not thy intereft *William Goddard.* [*Here I
could name gentlemen of reputation, of all denominations, who, in Mr.*
Wharton'*s opinion, were not to be trufted, who would be dangerous
companions, and no fervice to me in my ftation; but I do not defire to fubject Mr.* Wharton *to a corporal difcipline; for ' the fevereft punifhment
of an injury is the confcience of having done it; and no man fuffers
more, than he that is turned over to the pain of repentance.'*]

Goddard. Sir, I am difpofed to oblige you, to the utmoft of my
ability, confiftent with my reputation, but no farther will I proceed.

Wharton. *Thee talks* too much of *thy* reputation—what is *thy* reputation without us! *Thee ftands* on pundilios as much as if *thee
had* not a fortune to make. Upon the whole, *William,* we have confidered of this affair, and we are determined that it *fhall be fo.* It is
beft to be plain.

Goddard. Sir, as you think it is beft to be plain, and have been
fo, I hope you'll indulge me with equal freedom.

Wharton. By all means—I have no *interefted* views *William.*

Goddard. Then, Sir, I have confidered of this affair, and I
have determined it " fhall *not* be fo"—but I infift on going on agreeable to the articles between us.

Wharton.

Wharton. *William Goddard, thee knows* not OUR power. *Would thee* offer to contend with us ? I tell thee, whofoever WE fet up, is fet up—and whofoever we pull down, is pull'd down—therefore take care how *thee conducts* thyfelf.

Goddard. I have fo good an opinion of the benevolence and humanity of the inhabitants of *Pennfylvania*, as to believe they would not fuffer a man to be crufh'd or *pull'd down* by the hand of power.

Wharton. *Thee knows* not the people, nor thy true intereft. If *thee will* confent, we'll be thy friends.——But if *thee refufes, thee* art UNDONE. We will BREAK from thee, and will ruin thee. We can do it. We are able to crufh thee in a moment. We will now withdraw our fupport. We will no longer pay for paper, and thy *Chronicle* fhall fall, unlefs *thee confents* to our propofal.—Befides, we will have a prefs in oppofition to thee.

Goddard. Can you really mean, Sir, to take fuch an ungenerous advantage of me—and will you violate all your promifes ? How can you fet up a prefs in oppofition to me, when you have, under hand and feal, engaged not to do it ?

Wharton. *William, thee has* loft confidence in us, and it is no wonder we have loft confidence in thee. *Thee will* not call, as formerly, upon *Jofeph Galloway* and myfelf. A prefs we will have, and if we cannot be concerned in one immediately, we have intereft enough to get one eftablifhed.

Goddard. Your own conduct made your houfes intolerable—I have loft confidence in you, becaufe you have repeatedly deceived me by violating your engagements, in every important particular, and your lofs of confidence in me, arifes from your knowledge of my integrity.

Wharton. *Thee* art a very haughty infolent young man. Thy pride fhall be taken down. Mark my words !

Goddard. This is very extraordinary from M*r. Thomas Wharton !* Take care, Sir, that your pride does not meet with a fall—but nothing elfe, I fear, can poffibly fubdue your imperious difpofition, which makes every perfon connected with you unhappy.

Mr. *Wharton* grew more temperate upon this—but he ftill infifted on my complying with his propofal.

Upon a view of my cafe, and feeing that there was no dependance to be placed on my partners, I judged it prudent to amufe them with a notion that they fhould be gratified after a while. In the mean time, I offered to admit any perfon of their appointing to manage the books, which I thought fufficient, fubject to their infpection monthly or weekly. This condefcenfion in me prevented their taking an advantage of the particular fituation I was then in—and under an expectation of fpeedily gaining a *complete victory* over me, they appeared well fatisfied, became very civil and polite, pretending they were my *fincere friends*, and were difpofed to render me all the fervices in their power.

☞ *Numb.* II. *of this hiftory, is in the prefs, and will be publifhed as fpeedily as poffible.*

THE

PARTNERSHIP:

OR THE

HISTORY

OF THE

RISE AND PROGRESS

OF THE

PENNSYLVANIA CHRONICLE, &c.

NUMBER II.

IN *December* 1768, I went to *Rhode-Island*, for the collection of considerable debts due to me there, arising from business heretofore done in that colony, as also for the transaction of divers other interesting matters. Before I sat out, I acquainted my partners with my business, and they were, to appearance, well satisfied. — I provided the office with every thing necessary for the due prosecution of the business, and left it to the management of Mr. *Towne*, subject to the superior direction of Mrs. *Goddard.* — My partners having failed in supplying me with cash, agreeable to their promises, I was obliged, after the first year of the *Chronicle* was expired, to call upon my customers, who, in general, paid me with great honour and punctuality. These *disinterested* partners, who *only* meant " *to serve the public,*" well knew that in *January,* the next month, while I should be absent, several hundred pounds would become payable to me. They were determined, if possible, to *take care* of the money for me, thinking *their desks* more *safe* for it than *my own*; accordingly, they *kindly* advised my mother to pay all the cash she should receive, in my absence, to them, " *only for the sake of safety.*" This my mother could not be made to see the propriety of, she therefore appropriated it, agreeable to my request, to the discharge of the company debts, and the purchase of stock for the printing-office.

The materials that I brought here with me, were purchased by a friend to my family, to whom I gave a mortgage of an estate of greater
value,

D

value at *New-London.* This eſtate I was deſirous of ſelling, in order to pay my friend, being determined to appropriate no part of the company's money, beſore a ſettlement, to the diſcharge of any debt of my own—and to enable me to diſpoſe of it, for ſuch an honourable purpoſe, my mother cheerfully gave up her right of dower therein, upon my ſecuring to her a maintenance at *Philadelphia,* which I did by means of the printing-office. I inſert a copy of the inſtrument * in the margin, which we ſigned together, as from this tranſaction, which I did from a motive of duty, gratitude, juſtice, and filial affection, my enemies have collected a ſlander, and have charged me with ſomething baſe—but I ſhall take further notice of this inſtance of their cruelty and injuſtice, in a proper place — not doubting but their malice will recoil on their own heads.—Previous to my ſetting out on this journey, I engaged with Mr. *D—p,* on whoſe ſkill and accuracy I had a perfect reliance, to aſſiſt Mr. *Towne* in finiſhing the votes of the aſſembly, knowing the inſufficiency of my own materials. That portion of the work, which this gentleman undertook, he executed in ſuch a manner as reflects credit on him; but the ſeverity of the weather, and the nature of the work, (being the loan-office accounts for ſeventeen years) which required great care, would not permit him to finiſh them ſo early as it was expected. The expence of this, my

* *THIS INDENTURE, made the ſeventeenth day of* December, *one thouſand ſeven hundred and ſixty-eight, between* Sarah Goddard, *widow, of the city of* Philadelphia, *in the province of* Pennſylvania, *on the one part, and* William Goddard, *of ſaid* Philadelphia, *printer, on the other part, witneſſeth, that the ſaid* Sarah Goddard, *doth by theſe preſents, and for in conſideration of the grants and covenants hereafter expreſſed on the part of the ſaid* William, *grants to him the ſaid* William Goddard, *his heirs and aſſigns, all her right of dower to, and in all and ſingular which ſaid* William *now poſſeſſeth, as heir to his father* Giles Goddard, *Phyſician, late of* New-London, *in* New-England, *which the ſaid* Giles *was in his life time, and at the time of his death, the lawful huſband of ſaid* Sarah Goddard, *and father of ſaid* William Goddard : *And whereas the ſaid* Sarah Goddard, *held and poſſiſſed in partnerſhip with* William Goddard, *a printing-office at* Providence, *in* New-England, *with all the utenſils and appurtenances to the ſame belonging, which partnerſhip is ſince expired, and on adjuſtment of accounts between ſaid* Sarah *and* William, *there was, and is now, a balance of one hundred and nine pounds ſterling money due from ſaid* William *to ſaid* Sarah ; *and the ſaid* Sarah Goddard *doth by theſe preſents, for conſiderations hereafter mentioned, return to ſaid* William Goddard, *all the ſaid one hundred and nine pounds ſterling money, due to her on balance as aforeſaid ; and the ſaid* William, *in conſideration of the above grant and releaſe of ſaid* Sarah, *to him, for himſelf, his heirs, executors, and adminiſtrators, doth grant to ſaid* Sarah Goddard, *and her aſſigns, all that his printing-office which he now holds and occupies in the city of* Philadelphia, *together with all and ſingular the buſineſs, utenſils, ſtores of every kind, books, debts, and appurtenances whatever, in any and every manner*

my partners have fince refufed to pay any part, of, and it has finally
fallen upon me, to the amount of *£*. 25; and I know of no other relief than petitioning the General Affembly, to the difgrace of their
Speaker. I tarried in *New-England*, with a view to clofe my bufinefs
there, (as it was expected) near three months; but the great fcarcity
of money prevented my difpofing of my intereft at *New-London*, nor
could I get the money due to me for my printing-office, without injuring a young beginner, and doing as I would *not* be done by. I
found, on my return, that Mr. *Towne* had conducted the bufinefs very indifferently. He had done little elfe than the news-paper, and
that was executed in fo injudicious a manner, that I had the mortifica-
tion to hear it compared to " a large barn ftuffed with ftraw," and
was advifed never again to leave the SLEEPY GENIUS of Mr. *Towne*
to entertain the city of *Philadelphia*. I regulated the affairs of the
office, and put the votes in fuch forwardnefs, that they were com-
pleated,

manner arifen or arifing from incidents, and appertaining to faid laft-
mentioned printing-office, and printing bufinefs, in faid Philadelphia, *and*
that the faid Sarah *fhall and may, immediate'y, by force and virtue of thefe*
prefents, enter on, ufe, occupy, and enjoy, demand and receive all and fin-
gular the premifes to her own ufe and benefit, together with all and fingu-
lar the goods and eftates which the faid William Goddard *now poffeffeth,*
or hath a right to in Philadelphia, *and province of* Pennfylvania.———
  In witnefs whereof the faid Sarah *and* William Goddard *have here-*
unto fet their hands and feals the day and year above written.

SARAH GODDARD,   (L. S.)
WILLIAM GODDARD. (L. S.)

Signed, fealed and delivered
in the prefence of us,
  CALEB RICE,
  PETER HUGHES.

Before me the fubfcriber, one of his Majefty's Juftices, &c. came Peter
  Hughes, *one of the fubfcribing witneffes to the within indenture,*
  who being duly fworn on the Holy Evangelifts of Almighty God, did
  depofe and fay, that he was prefent and did fee the within named
  Sarah Goddard *and* William Goddard *feal, and, as their act and*
  deed, deliver the faid indenture, and that he did alfo fee Caleb
  Rice *fubfcribe his name as the other witnefs of fuch fealing and deli-*
  very, and that the name of Peter Hughes, *thereto fubfcribed as a wit-*
  nefs, is of his, this deponent's, own proper hand-writing, and further
  faith not.

(L. S.) *Sworn and fubfcribed to before me* ⎫ PETER HUGHES.
         this 1ft day of December, 1769.   ⎭
         JAMES HUMPHREYS.

Recorded in the office for recording of deeds, for the city and county of Philadelphia, *in book* I. *vol.* 6. *page* 554, &c.
          Certified under my hand and feal of office, this 29th
  (L. S.)   *day of* December, 1769.

WILLIAM PARR, *Record.* &c.

pleated, and not much out of feafon. If I miftake not, they were
finifhed before the rife of the affembly then fitting.

I had fcarcely refted from the fatigue of a long journey, before
Meffrs. *Galloway* and *Wharton* paid me a vifit, and BID mo a very
extraordinary *welcome*, by acquainting me, in an imperious manner,
that as I had acted fo *independent* of them, and had refufed to take in a
reprefentative of them into the office, they were determined no
longer to be connected with it, therefore *required* me either to buy or
fell, and demanded a CATEGORICAL ANSWER, declaring, if I refufed,
they would advertife me in the *Gazette*, blaft my credit, and complete my ruin. I expreffed my furprife at this precipitate *onfet*, and,
as it was a matter of great confequence, I afked how long they would
give me to determine thereon?—They *humanely* allowed me three
days. I told them that I fhould defpife myfelf if I fuffered any of
their threats to intimidate me into any mean compliances; but they
fhould hear from me foon, for I was heartily tired of a connexion
with them. Before they left my houfe, they thought it neceffary, to
cover their *real* defigns againft me, to find fault with my conduct in
not accounting with them exactly agreeable to the articles, and for a
trifling delay in printing the votes. Thefe were the only accu-
fations they had the *affurance* to make againft me before my mother;
and altho' I obviated every thing they fuggefted, in fuch a manner that
they could not fay one rational thing further on the fubject, that could
militate againft me, yet they were far from being fatisfied. In fact the
plot had been laid fome time before, to work me out of *my own* office,
or if they could not effect that immediately, to *force* their tool. Mr.
Towne, into it; and in cafe they failed in both, the; *undoubtedly* intended to fet him up in oppofition to me; for which laft purpofe, Mr.
Galloway had got a parcel of types in his own cellar, and Mr.
Towne had actually another parcel privately ftored in the city, tho'
he repeatedly denied it. My mother had paid away confiderable
fums in my abfence, and not apprehending any frefh hoftility from
my partners, had neglected to provide a proper ftock of paper. The
fituation of the office as to this particular, thro' Mr. *Towne*, (Meffrs.
Galloway and *Wharton*'s DAILY ADVERTISER) became well known.
They confidered this a glorious time to effect their purpofes.——
It was only refufing to perform their engagements to our paper-maker, and that would fo alarm him, that he would no longer fupply
me with paper, except I paid off the debt they had contracted; and I
could get no feafonable relief on this fide the atlantic, he being the only
man in *America*, who made fuch paper as I ufed. The reader will
eafily form an idea of this inhuman confpiracy, and the motives which
actuated its authors. I took Meffrs. *Galloway* and *Wharton*'s converfation and *demand* into confideration, and wrote them as follows,
viz.

Thurfday, March 8, 1769.

Meff's. GALLOWAY and WHARTON,

    GENTLEMEN,

    " I have ferioufly confidered your converfation laft evening, which,
as I recollect it, was to this purport:

" 1. That

" 1. That you infifted on being difengaged from your connexion in the printing-office, by obliging me either to buy your fhares, or fell my own to you.

" 2. That you were diffatisfied that the printing the affembly's votes was delayed, and therefore would not continue the affembly's bufinefs in the office.

" 3. That you were diffatisfied that the accounts of the office were not adjufted yearly, according to the articles.

" 4. That you propofed my taking a partner.

" 1. My anfwer is—To the firft by and by.

" 2. To the fecond, that the reafon of the delay was a deficiency of figure types in the office, to fet the unufual number of accounts inferted in thofe minutes, which made the printing of them in our office impracticable, and when put out to be done, the printer who was employed, could not complete them agreeable to the time fixed upon, which was without my knowledge, as I was out of town on bufinefs, to which you have not objected—And as thefe reafons of that particular delay may not happen again, I hope, on mature deliberation, you will not think there is fuch a prefumption of future delays, as will make it neceffary to apply to another office.

" 3. To the third, I own the deficiency is on my fide, but you muft be fenfible that I have many things to urge in my excufe, as my time was vaftly taken up in giving the bufinefs of the office its firft courfe, and putting all the parts in proper motion. My domeftic economy required my perfonal attendance—was a ftranger in the city, and not able to difpatch bufinefs quick, through ignorance of the cuftoms and courfe of the city, and the faces and abodes of men concerned, &c. all which reafons of delay are now removed, and I have time to beftow a more timely and particular attention to the bufinefs of the office, without fuch innumerable and unavoidable avocations as interrupted me in my firft beginnings.——But after all, the damage arifing from the delay of adjuftment of accounts, cannot be very confiderable, as thofe accounts will be the principal object of my attention, till they are adjufted and fettled to fatisfaction by all the partners.

" I now proceed to anfwer the firft particular, viz. about diffolving the partnerfhip. I well knew when I contracted with you, that it would be inconvenient for me to begin the partnerfhip for a continuance of lefs than fifteen years; otherwife I fhould not have contracted as I did. I am not at all fatisfied that you have any right to compel me to buy or fell; i. e. to give up the contract of the company; but, neverthelefs, would do it freely, inafmuch as you defire it, if I could do it without the greateft inconveniency to myfelf.——To buy I am not able; to fell would be to throw myfelf, my aged mother, and only fifter out of bread. At your repeated advice and folicitation, and blaming me when I objected, for feeming to want confidence in you, you well know, Gentlemen, I gave up my bufinefs at *Providence*, and brought my mother and fifter here, at confiderable expence, and with a view of fuch benefits arifing therefrom, as you yourfelves pointed out to me; nor did I think it poffible for you to take advantage of the particular fituation you yourfelves have brought me into, by your advice and influence with me, and my great confidence in you, to urge me to a measure which would either be impracticable or ruinous.——I know you are not, men I am either able or willing to contend with. If there is a single article of dispute between us, that we cannot settle amicably, I am content to refer it to the judgment of such as we can both trust; but to dissolve the partnership is out of my power. However, I will propose to you all I can do—If you will agree to continue your friendship and influence to the office, and not be concerned in promoting any other, and will accept my bond, payable in three years, for all the monies you have ever paid to the office, I will give you such a bond and release, and cancel the company articles.

" 4. As to the fourth particular, about a partner, I answer—If you will convey your shares to any printer, to whom I have no objection, (for I cannot be *forced* into a partnership with any person disagreeable to me) and who is able to carry on one half the business, I will accept such a partner, if he comes in in his *own right*, but not if he is placed there as your *deputy* or *agent*; for as long as I am in partnership with you, I insist on having the *sole* management of the office, according to our articles.

" These are all the answers I am able to make. I hope you will be satisfied with them, especially when you consider it is plainly out of my power to make any other. I am as willing to be unembarassed by you, as you can be to be rid of me; and if these answers give satisfaction, I shall rejoice heartily that I have been able *once* to please, and shall with great pleasure study to be agreeable to you, and will answer all the *salutary* purposes you *proposed* in forming a partnership with me. I am, Gentlemen, with all respect,
Your most humble servant,
WILLIAM GODDARD."

The above letter was inclosed in another, of which the following is a copy, viz.

March 8, 1769.

GENTLEMEN,

" I have, on the coolest deliberation, made my resolutions on the subject of our conversation last evening, which I here inclose to you; and, if agreeable, I beg the favour of your sentiments thereon in the same manner, in which there can be no room either for misunderstanding or misrepresentations of each other's sense, or for any imprudent word or passionate expression, which might arise from sudden resentments, of which I acknowledge myself capable, and not always sufficiently guarded against. I doubt not but your temper is open and unreserved enough to prevent your objecting to my proposal. Your compliance, Gentlemen, I shall esteem as an instance and proof of your just and generous sentiments towards, Gentlemen, your most humble servant, WILLIAM GODDARD."

Messrs. *Galloway* and *Wharton.*

The Gentlemen returned me for answer, " We *will not* write letters——no good end can be answered by writing letters."

My resolutions were very alarming to my partners.——They
apprehended

apprehended if I was firm, all their machinations would prove abortive, and they would be under a neceffity of rifking their own reputation, by endeavouring, as they threatened, to deitroy mine. Now or never, as they imagined, was their time ; for if I was fuffered to go on much longer, I fhould make myfelf entirely independent of them: they therefore watched opportunities, when I was abfent, to call upon my mother, to alarm her fears, by denouncing the moft terrific threats againft me ; fuch as thefe—that they would difgrace me, by taking the government's bufinefs out of my hands—that they would fue me for large fums of money—hold me to fuch bail that it was not probable I could get—advertife me in the papers—get fomebody to oppofe me—and, finally, that I fhould be *deftroyed, and that without remedy.* They magnified their great *power* and *importance,* and their fovereignty over the people and their reprefentatives, in fuch a ferious folemn way, that my mother was filled with all the painful apprehenfions and fenfations natural to the fondeft and moft affectionate of parents. To add ftill further to her fears, and to diftrefs me into a compliance with their propofals, they artfully contrived to offend two men to whom the company was indebted, and thereby provoked them to bring fuits againft me. I offered to pay my part of the refpective debts directly, and urged my partners to pay the reft—but they abfolutely refufed, as they did to be my bail, tho' one of the debts Mr. *Wharton* contracted himfelf—and when he was applied to for the money, he evaded payment, by faying that it could not be recovered of him, becaufe his name was not in my publications, and that I muft be fued firft. A pettifogger, who was inimical to me, being advifed with on the matter, I was fued without hefitation. But *Pennfylvania* was not deftitute of humanity. Gentlemen were foon found, who looked with an eye of abhorrence on fuch barbarity, and ftepped forth, in the moft difinterefled and honourable manner to my relief. Thefe unexpected *actions,* added to the ideas they had raifed in my mother's mind, induced her, as they expected, to prevail on me to give up the contract of the company, and permit them to fell out to Mr. *Towne.* I told her I was diffuaded from fuch a meafure by every other friend in the city, and hoped fhe would not infift upon my giving up my articles to men who had *fhaken hands and parted* with truth, honour and juftice, except I could be properly indemnified from their part of the company debts. She replied, that if I took in Mr. *Towne,* I fhould no longer be fubject to the caprices of Meffrs. *Galloway* and *Wharton,* —that Mr. *Towne* would never offer to controul me as they had done—that I fhould prevent an oppofition to me—that I fhould fecure the government's printing work, not through the friendfhip of my partners, but from motives of felf-intereft, as they were willing to take their pay of him, for their fhare, in that very work, and that they would free me from their part of the company debts—that thereby I fhould have their intereft as long, perhaps, as I fhould need it, and efcape a difagreeable and expenfive lawfuit, and all the trouble and perplexity that their malice and ill-will could bring upon me. To this fhe added——" I followed you to this province, with the pleaf-
" ing hopes of being a fpectator of your happinefs and profperity—
" Let

" Let not, I befeech you, all my fond hopes be blafted in an inftant.
" It is not for any worldly intereft that I fhould gain by it. My
" time is fhort—and were it not for a defire of feeing you happily
" fettled in life, I fhould wifh that I had the wings of a dove, that I
" might flee away and be at reft." The manner in which this was
delivered, caufed fuch emotions in my breaft, that I fuddenly promifed, upon the above conditions, to give up the articles of agreement. I could not refift the earneft entreaties of an infirm and aged
parent, I therefore confented to an act, the performance of which has
involved me in difficulties inexpreffible, and may prove my ruin in
the end. Before a diffolution of the partnerfhip could take place, the
accounts were to be fettled. I employed an accurate accomptant for
the ftating and preparing them for the infpection of their *High Migh-
tineffes*, which were done and prefented accordingly. In the mean
time, Mr. *Hagey*, our paper-maker applied to Meffrs. *Galloway* and
Wharton for the money they owed him. They refufed to pay him a
farthing, and advifed him to fue me for what they had engaged to
pay under their own hands, telling him that no money could be recovered of them, till he had *firft* fued me. In one of their letters to
Mr. *Hagey*, they faid they would not have him fail bringing paper,
one week, for the *Chronicle*, for £. 500. This honeft man was
fhocked at the injuftice of my partners, and refufed to be a means of
injuring a man who had always ufed him kindly, and threatened to
lay a complaint againft Mr. *Wharton*, before that fociety of which
he is an *unworthy* member. This lowered their tone, and they promifed he fhould have fatisfaction the next week. Mr. *Wharton* feeing
me in the ftreet, near his ftore, the fame day, addreffed me with his
ufual civility—" *William Goddard*, I have fomething of moment to
impart to thee—ftep hither." I went into his ftore, where ftrutting
between a rum puncheon and a melaffes tierce, in the plenitude of
his imaginary *power* and *importance*, and with as much affected *dignity* as if he had a *ducal coronet* on his head, he infifted I fhould pay off
the debt he and Mr. *Galloway* had contracted with Mr. *Hagey*. He faid
I had a great deal of money due, and that I *muft* and *fhould* collect it. I
told him, that as he and his friend Mr. *Galloway* had taken an ungenerous advantage of me, and would not pay their part of other company debts, even fuch as were of their *own immediate contracting*, in order to reduce me to difhonourable terms of fettlement, I would not
pay a farthing of that particular debt; efpecially as they had *caufed
fuits to be brought againft me, and refufed to be my bail*. We then had
a frefh dialogue, which I here infert, becaufe any thing from *fuch a
genius* as Mr. *Thomas Wharton*, fenior, can't fail of *entertaining* the
public.

Wharton. *William Goddard*, we have thee in our power. Thee
art *prefumptuous* to oppofe us. I know *thee* art out of paper. We have
refufed to pay *Hagey*, and he will no longer fupply thee—thy *Chronicle* fhall fall, and then what will become of thee ?—If *thee will* take
upon thee our debt, *thee can* eafily collect £. 300, we will be thy
friends, and will ftill ferve thee.

Goddard. Upon the fettlement of accounts, if I owe you any
thing,

thing, I will pay you; but I cannot engage to pay a sum beyond my ability. 'Tis unreasonable—'tis unjust, Sir.

Wharton. WE have considered of this matter, *William*. and we *will not* be put off. *We will* OBLIGE *thee to pay this man!*

Goddard. Mr. *Wharton*, I will give you an order for near £. 100, on the treasury, and will endeavour to collect a further sum, to oblige you, in a little time, but I *cannot do more*.

Wharton. This will not satisfy us. *Thee shall* comply, or depend upon it, *thee shall* recent thy refusal.

Goddard. Mr. *Wharton*, you press me too hard.——'Tis cruel and ungenerous beyond compare.

Wharton. I declare to *thee*, *William*, we will not give up this point; we will UNDO thee if *thee does* not comply. .

Goddard. This is *harsh language* from a partner. I can endure it no longer.——Mr. *Wharton*, your behaviour to me is insufferable, and I *declare* to YOU, that if you proceed in any *undue* measures to injure my interest and reputation, as I am not a man of fortune to contend in a *legal* way, I *must* and I *will* take my own PERSONAL SATISFACTION.

At this the *hero* stood aghast——and the dialogue ceased.

He flew to Mr. *Galloway*, and related the *unpardonable* treatment he had met with. Mr. *Galloway* posted away to my house, and, with a *flattering obsequiousness*, told me he was *very sorry* for what had happened between Mr. *Wharton* and me, but that he was a hasty warm man, and I should not resent his *rude* behaviour, which was a *constitutional* failing of his. He then proposed to set down with me that evening, and lay a foundation for an *amicable* settlement; he was *sure* we should agree, and that he always believed me to be an upright man. Ever willing to attend to any reasonable proposition, I consented with pleasure. We spent the evening together, and hit upon this plan of settlement—I was to permit my partners to sell their share in the printing-office to Mr. *Towne*. They were to take their pay in the profits arising from the government's printing work, and were to use all their interest for the office as usual, and that they would pay, or enable Mr. *Towne* to pay, their part of the company debts, so that I should be no sufferer. Upon these conditions, which I thought fair and equitable, I consented to cancel the articles of *Galloway*, *Wharton*, and *Goddard*. The evening closed much to my satisfaction, and I began to anticipate the dawn of freedom. As I could not bear the incivility of Mr. *Wharton*, which Mr. *Galloway* well knew, it was agreed, that my mother should be impowered to settle and adjust all matters of account between us, and render void all agreements. I gave my mother a power* for that purpose, from a hearty disposition to part in friendship, notwithstanding all that had past, and she, Mr. *Wharton* and Mr. *Towne*, met on the business.

E   Mr.

---

* *KNOW ALL MEN by these presents*, that I William Goddard, *of the city of* Philadelphia, *Printer*, *having made, ordained and constituted, and by these presents do make, ordain and constitute, and in*

my

Mr. *Galloway*, being indifposed, could not attend. Mr. *Wharton* made many abfurd objections to my accounts, infifting that I could not have ufed fo much wood as I charged, becaufe *he* did not, nor fo many candles, becaufe *he* did not, &c. &c.————He was, upon the whole, fo *troublefome* and *arbitrary*, that my mother gave up the bufinefs, much difappointed, and requefted me to lay afide all refentment, and, if poffible, put an end to fuch a *flavifh connexion*. I judged it beft to do fo, and therefore propofed a meeting to Mr. *Wharton*, affuring him that I was difpofed to bury every thing that had paft between us in oblivion. He attended in a *feeming* good humour. We fat down, and went over the accounts line by line. He foon began to knit his brows, and to twift in his chair. He then found fault with, and abufed a worthy gentleman who ftated the accounts, and made the fame objections that he had before done. I told him, in fhort, that they were juft and true—that I had vouchers for all confiderable

———————————————————————

my place and ftead put and depute my trufty and loving friend and mother Sarah Goddard; my true and lawful attorney, for me, and in my name, and for my ufe, to afk, demand, fue for, recover and receive all fuch fum and fums of money, debts, goods, wares, dues, accounts, and all other demands whatfoever, which are or fhall be due, owing, payable and belonging to me, or detained from me by any manner of ways or means whatfoever, by any perfon or perfons whatfoever, and alfo for me and in my name to adjuft, fettle, and finally determine all accounts, and to difannul and make void all agreements of whatfoever kind or nature now or at any time heretofore entered into and fubfifting between me and Jofeph Galloway, Efq; and Thomas Wharton, merchant, giving and granting unto my faid attorney, by thefe prefents, my full and whole power, ftrength and authority in and about the premifes, to have, ufe and take all lawful ways and means, in my name, for the recovery thereof. And upon the receipt of any fuch debts, dues or fums of money aforefaid, acquittances, or other fufficient difcharges, for me and in my name, to make, feal and deliver. And generally, all and every other act or acts, thing and things, device and devices in the law whatfoever needful and neceffary to be done in and about the premifes, for the recovery of all or any fuch debts or fums of money aforefaid, for me and in my name to do, execute and perform, as fully, largely and amply, to all intents and purpofes, as I myfelf might or could do, if I was perfonally prefent, or as if the matter required more fpecial authority than is herein given. And attornies, one or more under me for the purpofe aforefaid, to make and conftitute, and again at pleafure to revoke. Ratifying, allowing, and holding for firm and effectual all and whatfoever my faid attorney fhall lawfully do in and about the premifes by virtue hereof. In Witnefs whereof I have hereunto fet my hand and feal, this twelfth day of May, Annoque Domini, 1769.

WILLIAM GODDARD. (L. S.)

Signed, fealed and delivered
in the prefence of
ROBERT LEVERS,
MARY LEVERS.

derable fums of money, and that I would not fubmit to any of his arbitrary objections; but if he could point out any real miftakes, in a decent gentlemanlike manner, I would rectify them with the greateft
pleafure imaginable. A complaifant behaviour to fuch a man, was
like cafting pearls before fwine.—Nothing would ferve him but *fubmiffion to his will*. He had found that there was a balance due to me
from himfelf and Mr. *Galloway*, he was therefore determined to object to and erafe out of my accounts as much as would bring a balance
in their favour; for he had told in many companies that I was deeply
in their debt.——High words were like to be the refult of this meeting—to prevent which, and to effect fome kind of fettlement, my
mother interpofed, and begged to be admitted as a mediator. She
obferved, that we both loved to have our own way fo well, that fhe
faw no probability of our fettling the accounts accurately, fhe therefore propofed a fettlement in grofs, without going thro' the particular articles, and recommended to me to give up the balance due to
me, *for the fake of peace*; and, if I would, fhe engaged to make up
the lofs to me; that Mr. *Towne* might then come in, if Mr. *Wharton* and he could agree, and be entitled to one moiety of whatever
monies were due to the office, and be liable to pay one moiety of
whatever monies were due from the office. Mr. *Wharton* readily
agreeing to this, I made no objection. A minute was made of this
agreement, and the accounts were thrown afide. Mr. *Wharton* appeared highly pleafed, and a reconciliation feemed to have taken place,
and he was *liberal* with his *wifhes* for my profperity. Mr. *Towne* then
agreed to give Meffrs. *Galloway* and *Wharton* £. 572 for their fhare,
the amount of what they furnifhed, from time to time, in money, and
new and *old* furniture; but as Mr. *Towne* had engaged to put his
printing materials into ftock, and had fome wages due to him, tho'
I paid him more money than ever he earned, I further confented to
lighten his debt, by giving my obligation for £. 46, payable alfo in the
government's printing-work. Mr. *Wharton* then went away to prepare the writings. The fame day, the 19th of *May*, he bro't the new
articles to be figned by Mr. *Towne* and me. On perufing them, I found
they were improperly drawn, being very ambiguous and obfcure in
feveral places, and apparently calculated to *conceal* the firft partnerfhip. I objected to them in the ftrongeft terms, and fain would have
had a conveyancer fent for, to draw up a new fet; but Mr. *Wharton* begged that nobody might have any fhare in, or knowledge of,
thefe tranfactions, left the *company fecrets* fhould, by any means, be
difclofed; and I was finally *prevailed* on to fign them, which I did
the more readily, in order to efcape the gripe of *arbitrary power*. Mr.
Towne was, by the new articles, put into the place of Meffrs. *Galloway*
and *Wharton*, and confidered a partner from *January* 1767, and the
partnerfhip was to continue till *January* 1782, and he was entitled to
receive and liable to pay as they were; and they, by their *folemn engagements*, became his fecurities. Thefe articles were witneffed by
Mrs. *Goddard*, and Mr. *Wharton*, becaufe my partners were *afraid* and
afhamed to have any other perfon acquainted with their proceedings.
Immediately after figning them, while they lay on the table, Mr.

Wharton

Wharton, inſtead of exchanging our articles, in an honeſt way, ſuddenly took mine out of my mother's hand, as ſhe was reading them, and *inſtantaneouſly* tore them, with his own, into pieces, and burnt them, ſaying, " *It is beſt to put theſe out of the way.*" I mentioned the impropriety of his conduct, in deſtroying our articles, before I had received a proper diſcharge from him and Mr. *Galloway*. He ſaid, " *William Goddard*, I am thy friend, and do not intend to hurt thee, and *thee ſhall* have a diſcharge whenever *thee will* call upon *Joſeph Galloway* and myſelf—It is proper that we both ſign ſuch a writing." The ſolemn promiſes of Mr. *Wharton*, having induced my mother to think I was in no danger, I gave up the matter.

Mr. *Wharton* then produced a bond for Mr. *Towne* to ſign, for £. 526, payable in one year, without any mention being made of the money being payable in printing work. A bond for me, for £. 46, was alſo prepared, in like manner. As a friend I told Mr. *Towne*, it was very unſafe for him to ſign ſuch a bond. He replied, that he ' *had confidence in the gentlemen.*' Mine was ſo ſmall a ſum, I did not regard it. Mr. *Wharton* obſerved, that it would not be *proper* to mention the government's buſineſs in the bonds, as it might poſſibly be a *diſadvantage* to " friend *Galloway*," tho' we might depend on having it, and that they had no expectation of getting their money in any other manner than from the provincial treaſury.

On this occaſion, Mr. *Wharton*, by making ſtrong aſſurances of friendſhip, and engaging to render my family and me all the good offices in his power, prevailed on my mother and me, to join with Mr. *Towne* in a bond for £. 130, payable to our papermaker, which, with what I paid ſoon after, relieved him and Mr. *Galloway* from a debt, of their contracting, of near £. 300—This being done, Mr. *Wharton* engaged to go *immediately* and ſtop thoſe actions that he had been the means of bringing upon me, and to enable Mr. *Towne* to perform his engagements; which if he had done, my affairs would have been in a proſperous ſituation. As it became the intereſt of Meſſrs. *Galloway* and *Wharton* to ſerve the office, not penetrating their latent purpoſes, and that my new partner was in league againſt me, I thought myſelf ſafe, and felt happy that I had got out of *the houſe of bondage*—and all my friends participated with me on the occaſion.

Having buſineſs in *Maryland*, I ſat out on a journey thither, leaving the management of every thing in the printing-houſe to Mr. *Towne*, while my mother and ſiſter kept the books, diſpatched the papers, &c. During my abſence, on the 6th of *June*, Meſſrs. *Wharton* and *Towne* came to my mother with a *new ſtate* of the old *cancelled* accounts, pretending that as there was a balance due to me on my book, from Meſſrs. *Galloway* and *Wharton*, that Mr. *Towne* was liable to pay it, altho' we had ſettled in another way, (of which there was a minute made in the book) directly under the balance; and they induced my mother to ſign a certain certificate, that Mr. *Wharton* had prepared to her hand, by virtue of the power of attorney I had given her for the ſettlement of accounts, [ſee p. 33—34] altho' I had rendered that power *void* by my own act. This my mother knew;
yet

yet as they reprefented to her, that it was *only* to put matters on a *fair footing*, fhe ran the venture to act upon a power I had forgot to deftroy, not imagining that I was to be brought in debt by that means. But, in truth, Mr. *Wharton* had ftated the accounts in fuch a manner, that my mother was *deceived*; for I was actually made indebted to the printing office to the amount of *Two Hundred Pounds*, one half of which, in confequence of Mr. *Towne*'s purchafe, became his property. This was a capital ftroke, and made ample amends, for my refufing to permit Mr. *Wharton* to alter my accounts to fuit his pleafure. Nothing more, they thought, was wanting, but to get hold of my power of attorney. To effect which, Mr. *Towne*, the next day, when he came to dinner at my houfe, where he boarded, begg'd the favour of my mother to let him look at the power. Not fufpecting any wicked defign, fhe cheerfully complied with his requeft. He had no fooner gained it than he fuddenly rofe up, and carried it off to Mr. *Parr*'s, the recorder of deeds, and defired it might be immediately put on record, in order to give validity to the certificate Mr. *Wharton* and he had obtained by *deception*. Mr. *Parr* refufed to record it, as it was not acknowledged. Mr. *Towne* was then in great confufion. He prefs'd it without delay to the fecretion, and requefted them to acknowledge it; but they virtuoufly refufed, apprehending a fraud, as they knew the caufe for which it had been given, and that I had rendered it a mere *nullity*. Thus I efcaped. I foon returned, and hearing of this extraordinary affair, I went to Mr. *Parr*'s office, and by a certain inftrument now on record, I invalidated the power. I then demanded it of Mr. *Towne*. He made many mean evafions, to cover his bafe conduct, and declared that Mr. *Wharton* had got it. I was fo provoked, that I told him that if it was not delivered up, I would *handle* him and Mr. *Wharton* as they deferved. He then threatened to fwear the peace againft me, and pretended that he was going to a magiftrate's. I watched his motions, and found that, after walking round two or three fquares, he retreated into a gin-fhop, where I left him to ftifle the anguifh of *a guilty confcience.*—I then went to Mr. *Wharton*'s, but he did not incline to have another *dialogue* with me. Mr. *Galloway*, when I could *catch* him, told me, that as he was indifpofed, he had left all our affairs to be fettled by Mr. *Wharton*, for whofe conduct he was not accountable. I replied, that he was interefted in the bufinefs, and it was his duty to interfere, that I might obtain juftice, and that I expected not only the performance of the promifes that were made me on the day our partnerfhip ended, but a fpeedy return of the power. Mr. *Galloway* again made me fair promifes. but never performed one. Mr. *Towne* appeared before I left Mr. *Galloway*, and tho' he had pretended he only wanted to be *fafe*, he now began to *boaft* of his advantage, which he refufed to give up. I offered him an indemnification, that he fhould not be made to pay any part of the balance which Mr. *Wharton* infinuated he was liable to pay. Mr. *Galloway*, at length, finding me determined to expofe this black affair, told Mr. *Towne* he *muft* give up the power. He reluctantly confented to do it, upon my promifing to give him a proper indemnification. I wrote, one, which was corrected and approved of by Mr. *Galloway*, and en-

C   tered

tered it on the back of the articles in my hands, expecting Mr. *Towne* would do the same, and execute them according to promise; but, after consulting *privately* with Messrs. *Galloway* and *Wharton*, he evaded the performance, from day to day, and still detained the power.

The creditors of the company hearing of our disputes, pressed *me* to pay *all* the company debts. I offered to pay *my* part immediately, but that was not generally satisfactory. I applied to Mr. *Towne* to pay his part. He told me he had *nothing*. I reminded him of his telling me that he could raise £. 300, and that he would put his printing materials into stock. He then said, " *My money I have sent home—and my materials are disposed of.*" I then went to Messrs. *Galloway* and *Wharton*—but the *slight ties* ties of their *word* and *honour* would not bind them. They refused to pay a farthing, saying, " *We have done with the business—you and Mr.* Towne *must pay as well as you can.*"— Not knowing that I had a copy of the original articles of agreement, they were so hardy as to deny that any ever existed; and Mr. *Towne* frequently told me, with a sneer, that if they ever did exist, I could not *prove* it.——Both my mother and myself repeatedly wrote to Messrs. *Galloway* and *Wharton*, but our applications were in vain—not a line would they write, nor pay a farthing. We then applied, in like manner, to Mr. *Towne*, who, with a pitiful apery of his masters, acquainted us, that *he* too could " see no advantage in writing letters," and affected to be equally apprehensive of danger in putting pen to paper. I was, by this means, obliged to pay away almost all the cash I had laid by for the purchase of stock, in order to satisfy the creditors, many of whom, upon a proper representation of the case, behaved with the greatest generosity and humanity, while others, who were under the influence of Messrs. *Galloway* and *Wharton*, harrassed me beyond measure. They told me, in general, that my late partners would pay nothing, and as for Mr. *Towne*, they could only look upon him as my journeyman. In this situation, I was obliged to exert myself to the utmost of my ability, to save my credit, which the conduct of Messrs. *Galloway*, *Wharton*, and *Towne* had greatly impaired. I was not altogether unsuccessful, thro' the readiness of my customers to pay me. I was very ambitious to settle every thing in an honourable manner, as I had occasion to leave the province, and I did not choose to do it under any embarrassment, by whatever means occasioned. Considering Mr. *Galloway* a more rational man than either Mr. *Wharton*, or Mr. *Towne*, I sent him the following letter, *viz.*

" S I R,

" Mr. *Towne* having in the most shameful manner violated his engagements to my mother, relative to the power of attorney, and, in effect, refused to do any thing in the affairs of Mr. *D*— and Mr. *C*—, though they both make fair and equitable proposals, I must once more (need I say once for all ?) trouble you with my earnest request that something may be immediately done by you and Mr. *Wharton* in those several matters. I have now waited two months for justice to be done me, without seeking relief from any but the parties concerned; and I sincerely hope I shall not, *at last*, be under the painful

necessity

neceffity of bringing my copartnerfhip affairs, with my partners, before the bar of juftice and the public. I entreat your anfwer by the bearer, and am, Sir, your humble fervant,

Jofeph Galloway, Efq;   WILLIAM GODDARD."

Mr. *Galloway* returned me a verbal anfwer, that it was his determined refolution to write no letters, that he had not forgot that Governor *Franklin's* letters were exhibited in a public paper.

The time was now arrived when my bufinefs called me to *Providence*—but I was refolved never to leave this province till I had obtained the power of attorney that was unjuftly detained from me. My mother advifed me to write a polite note to Mr. *Wharton*, which I did, entreating him to do me the juftice to caufe the power to be returned, and to remember his promifes, refpecting the company debts. My mother alfo wrote to the fame purport. Her letter was treated with a contemptuous filence; but I received an abufive meffage in reply. This was delivered me as I was returning from a gentleman's country feat on the *Moyamenfing* road; but before the meffenger had finifhed, I faw Mr. *Wharton's* chariot, or *conveniency*, approach. I knew he was in it, and being fired with refentment at his inpudence and injuftice, I determined to ftop him, if poffible, and to duck him in one of the ditches on the road fide. I went back to a lane, where I expected he would turn down, and pofted myfelf in a proper manner for his reception; but finding that he had *ladies* with him, I could only tell him that the firft time I met him out of the company of the *fair*, I would WRING HIS NOSE. This I diftinctly repeated three times. He cry'd out to his fervant, " *drive on—drive on I tell thee*,"—and when he had got at a convenient diftance, he denounced a threat, and purfued his *flight*. I have been the more particular in my relation of this matter, as Meffrs. *Galloway* and *Wharton* have reprefented the affair in a falfe light; but I am able to prove that it happened exactly as I have related. When I got home, I related the adventure to my mother, and fent the following letter, which I haftily wrote, to Mr. *Galloway* :

" SIR,

" When Mr. *Wharton* was at my houfe, on the 19th of *May*, he promifed, as he acted, both for you and himfelf, on the word and honour of a gentleman, that in cafe I would amicably fettle and cancel all affairs of the partnerfhip, which I then did, you and he would fo manage matters, with the creditors of the company, particularly Mr. *D*— and Mr. *C*—, that I (who was only partly concerned) fhould fuffer no manner of inconvenience, or embarraffment therefrom—After waiting many weeks, (much to my prejudice) no one ftep has been taken to relieve me, but every poffible method made ufe of to diftrefs me ; nor will the *auguft* Mr. *Wharton* even deign to give an anfwer to letters, conceived in the civileft terms, if I *prefume* to remind him of his folemn engagements—engagements that would have been held facred by any perfon who had a grain of honour, or a fingle idea of a gentleman. And as from his late fraudulent conduct, in the affair of the power, I have no hopes of obtaining even common juftice from him, I muft once more trouble you with my earneft requeft,

that

that not only Mr. *D—t*'s and Mr. *C*—'s affairs may be somehow immediately settled, according to agreement, but that my papers may be
delivered me. All I ask is justice (I neither desire nor expect favour
from those whose tender mercies I have found to be cruelty) and if
I obtain it without further procrastination, I shall be content, even
under the base treatment I have unmeritedly received; but if, on the
contrary, I am still put off, and no notice taken of my equitable demands, I shall pursue such measures as I think proper for the preservation of my business and character, the ruin of which seems to be
aimed at, not doubting but it would involve my enemies in that infamy with which they have long laboured to overwhelm me. I will,
in short, let you know my determination—First I shall apply to council *learned in the law*, to know whether the *forcing* a man into partnership with me in your place, a man who is not worth a single sous,
will screen you from the payment of your own debts and contracts,
and whether, by such an artifice, I can be made to discharge all the
debts of the company.——For my part, when I take a review of all
the transactions past, I am in doubt whether the imposition is greater
on the public or myself, and therefore I am resolved to lay a complete state of the case before that tribunal, from the commencement
of the *first partnership* to Mr. *Wharton's coup de main*,—the sudden destruction of the articles, and the introduction of Mr. *Towne*, with a
copy of the articles duly authenticated—also remarks—anecdotes—
affidavits of my partners urging our creditors to sue me, to screen
themselves—ridiculous accusations—threats to ruin me—cabals held
with my journeymen—singular orders respecting my conduct—promises never fulfilled—ungenerous proposals, &c. &c. affording a
striking view of *disinterestedness—public spirit—patriotism—justice—
honour* and *humanity*.——This I will do with the greatest freedom to the parties concerned, and " nothing extenuate, or set down
ought in malice."——I shall also *take the liberty* to publish an advertisement, calling upon all persons indebted to *Joseph Galloway*, Esq;
Thomas Wharton, and *William Goddard*, PRINTERS, to make immediate payment, as the partnership is now dissolved, the latter being
determined to prosecute his business under no other favour and influence than the public's; for that no man could long keep himself or
press free with such connexions as I have unfortunately had. I shall
also notify the creditors of the said *Joseph Galloway*, Esq; *Thomas
Wharton*, and *William Goddard*, to produce their accounts for settlement.——Thus, Sir, have I hastily scrawled over my designs, which
I have not done, after the manner of your *worthy* colleague, to force
measures, but as an evidence of fair, open plain dealing. On such an
event, I know you would *arm* yourselves against me—and endeavour
to cut me off from the face of *Pennsylvania*—but I am too well acquainted with the *discipline* of your forces, to be apprehensive of any
thing very disastrous to me—yet, nevertheless, I am willing to bury
every thing in oblivion, if I can have but *bare justice* done your humble servant, WILLIAM GODDARD."

" *Joseph Galloway*, Esq;"

The

The next evening, *(Sunday)* Meſſrs. *Galloway* and *Wharton*, diſ-covering that I was abroad, paid my mother a viſit, and begged her to prevail upon me to proceed no further, and promiſed that the power ſhould be delivered me, and the company affairs be ' *properly managed.*' The next day, the power was delivered up, with confuſion of face, to my mother, by Mr. *Towne*, who was *permitted* to relieve me from a debt of Meſſrs. *Galloway* and *Wharton*, amounting to about £. 40, which, however, he has never yet diſcharged. They alſo left a certain writ-ing at my houſe, which they called a proper diſcharge. I did not ac-cept it as ſuch—But I was obliged to take that or none. They echoed their own praiſe, for doing *all this*, hoping to make people believe that they had done me ample juſtice.

By a perſeverance that would have done me credit with, and have gained me ſome quarter from a *generous enemy*, I removed every em-barraſſment that aroſe from my connexions here, and put my affairs upon a reſpectable footing—But a freſh misfortune aroſe, which gave my enemies all the pleaſures of a brutal triumph, ſuitable to their diſpoſitions. A demand was, by miſtake, made, in the abſence of my friend, who was in *Holland*, by his agent, for the money due to him for my materials, upon a ſuppoſition that I had made a fortune by my partnerſhip with Meſſrs. *Galloway* and *Wharton*. I was thereby in danger of being ſued for a ſum of money as a book-debt, when I had (voluntarily) given a deed of an eſtate as ſecurity, which, if I had paid the money, could not have been reconveyed to me in the abſence of my friend ; beſides, by taking a ſecurity in a deed, the book account was merg'd, and could not, by law, be recovered on account, but muſt be had on the deed, which was of a higher nature.—This circumſtance, added to my other concerns in *New-England*, obliged me to repair thither immediately ; and as I expected my friend would arrive before I returned, I was determined to ſell my intereſt at *New-London*, collect my debts in *Rhode Iſland*, pay for my materials, and bring the re-mainder of my money here, for the ſupport of my buſineſs, while the con-tinual income ariſing therefrom, would enable me to diſcharge Meſſrs. *Galloway* and *Wharton*'s debts, as well as my own. Before I ſat out, I employed a capable man to manage my buſineſs (as an overſeer of the printing-houſe) as I could not place any confidence in Mr. *Towne*, and gave him a power of attorney,* for that purpoſe ; and ſo deter-
F   mined

mined was I to get clear of him as soon as I could, that I never, or
any occasion, that I remember, united my name with his, under the
firm of the partnership. I thought it disgraceful to me. I chose rather to give obligations in my own name, and to be liable to pay, out
of my own private purse, all the debts I should contract for the office, than to do business with a tool of Messrs. *Galloway* and *Wharton*,
one

---

rage in his absence the said printing business, which is now under the di-
rection, care and circumspection of the said William Goddard—*Now*
know ye, that the said William Goddard, *reposing special trust and confi-*
dence in the diligence, integrity and ability of Theophilus Coslart, *of the*
said city, Printer, hath deputed, authorized, impowered, nominated,
constituted, appointed, and desired—and by these presents doth depute, au-
thorise, impower, nominate, constitute, appoint and desire the said
Theophilus Coslart, *in the absence, and until the return of him*
the said William Goddard *from the said government of* Rhode-
Island, *for him the said* William Goddard, *and in his name and*
stead to superintend, manage and direct all the concerns in the print-
ing-office in which the said William Goddard, *is concerned with*
Benjamin Towne, *as aforesaid, so far as relates to the printing the*
Pennsylvania Chronicle, *and all other printing-business to be done*
in the said office, in as full a manner as he the said William Goddard, *might or could do if he were personally present——And the said*
Theophilus Coslart, *is by these presents, by the said* William Goddard,
put in full possession of the said printing-office, with all the materials and
stock therein, and hereby authorized to receive all letters and news-papers
from the post-office, and every thing else belonging to the said William
Goddard, *the more effectually to enable him the said* Theophilus Coslart
to prosecute the said printing-business with proper skill and judgment—
And altho' the mode of printing the Pennsylvania Chronicle, *with the*
several pieces of intelligence, improvement and entertainment to be weekly
published therin, is at present, and for some time to come, will be under
the immediate sole direction of the said William Goddard—*he, the said*
Theophilus Coslart, *is directed to publish the same in* concert *and in* harmony *with the said* Benjamin Towne—*But if any undue measures*
shall or may be taken at any time in the absence of the said William Goddard, *to suppress the regular publication of the* Pennsylvania Chronicle,
or to insert any thing therein, contrary to the original free and impartial
plan of the said paper, the said Theophilus Coslart *is hereby fully au-*
thorized to superintend, direct and regularly to publish the said paper,
agreeable to the proposals of the said William Goddard, *weekly every*
Monday, against all opposition. *In witness whereof I the said*
William Goddard, *have hereunto set my hand and seal, the sixteenth of*
July, *one thousand seven hundred and sixty-nine.*

WILLIAM GODDARD, (L. S.)

Sealed and delivered in
the presence of
SHEPARD KOLLOCK,
THOMAS UPDIKE FOSDICK.

one whom I had taken into my bofom, and who had made me feel the venom of his fting.

I had no fooner left *Philadelphia*, than my enemies very induftri-oufly employed themfelves in traducing my character, by the moft cruel and unjuft reprefentations of my conduct and affairs, circulated in malignant whifpers here, and by anonymous letters, difpatched by poft, into other provinces, where I had lived with reputation, with-out having a fingle enemy.

To fhew my readers the extreme malice and inhumanity of the men, and that they would flick at nothing, however infamous in its nature, to invade my happinefs, and accomplifh my ruin, while they could act under a *vifor*, and thereby efcape detection, need I give any more demonftrative evidence, than a copy of one of their anony-mous letters, wrote to a gentleman, whofe daughter they only *ima-gined* I was under an engagement to?—The difcerning reader will perceive, that my difpute with Meffrs. *Galloway* and *Wharton*, and the embaraffments they threw upon me, were made the foundation of that extraordinary letter; and they will as eafily difcover the au-thor, and his principles, when I tell them that I had, on an acciden-tal interview with the gentleman to whom it was fent, on a former journey, recommended Mr. *Wharton*, as a proper perfon to tranfact bufinefs on commiffion, and to whom he might fafely fend a cargo, *&c.* by which means Mr. *Wharton* actually gained a confiderable fum, and that it was dated near the time I was about to humble his pride, by tumbling him into a ditch. The letter was *verbatim* as fol-lows, *viz.*

"*Philad: June* 28 1769

"Sir,

"It is *reported* here that Mr. *Godard* the Printer of the *Chronicle* is Courting and likely to be Married to one of your Daughters I am Sr a perfect Stranger to you both but haveing heard of your good Character I think it my duty juft to fay that its the *General Opinion* here he was fett up by two of our Principal ———— * Men but that this Conduct has been fuch that they have broke + from him--fo that he is now fued by his Journymen and others--in fhort if Your Daughter marries him fhe is Undone ‡—this hint will be fufficient for a tender Parent to make Inquirey from——*Its faid* he is very plaufable but that he is One of the moft unhappy and violent Tempers living—— I am Yr Hum. St. ————"

To G—— S—— ‖

This letter was properly directed, and was ftampt at the Poft-Office in this city, (30 IV.)

Much as the bafe author of this letter was miftaken in his informa-
ti n,

---

* *The word* gentlemen *was here erafed.*
† *See dialogue p.* 24.   ‡ *Ibid. p.* 24.
‖ *Though the ftyle of this letter is manifeftly adopted to conceal the author, yet a proper confiftency is not preferved to the laft, for the writer, in his zeal, forget to add the gentleman's addrefs, having, on other occa-fions, no doubt, been ufed to write without any.*

tion, refpecting the lady he alludes to, fuch a letter, on *fuch a fubjeEt*, written to a gentleman of reputation, a friend to me and my family, could not fail of giving me very fenfible concern, as I could not, with any propriety, offer to enter into a juftification of myfelf, where perh ips it might have been neceffary. Having accidentally heard of it, and the contents, while I was in *Rhode-Ifland*, and thinking it one of the moft fingular occurrences that ever had happened in *America*, I communicated it to my mother, as a proof of the unparalleled induftry of my enemies. My mother wrote me in anfwer as follows :

" MY DEAR SON,

" I am amazed at what you tell me, refpecting an anonymous letter being fent to ——— ———, to injure your reputation.— 'Tis an inftance of bafenefs, and depravity of foul, that fhocks me beyond expreffion. That a man fhould be guilty of writing what he dares not fign, is a degree of cowardice and meannefs that makes the author exceedingly contemptible.—But let it be your confolation— the charges againft you are falfe.—Continue to act uprightly, and this ill-will that you have experienced, will terminate to your advantage in the end, to the confufion of your enemies.—Put on good refolutions, and look up to a gracious God, to enable you to perform and perfe- vere.—As to your difpute with Meffrs. *Galloway* and *Wharton*, you fettled all matters between you, to the fatisfaction of all parties, as I thought, I am fure it was to mine, without any quarrel or paffion.— As to your journeymen fuing you, I know of but one, and he was hired by Mr. *Wharton*, and you faid he ought to pay him ; but as he worked in your office, and he fued you.—Let revenge, ill-will, and all fuch ignoble paffions, that live and fubfift in fuch diabolical natures, be forever put far from you and me ; and while your enemies tor- ment themfelves, by indulging fuch fhameful, wicked and fcandalous tempers, let us act with a fpirit of love, and pity thofe who are mak- ing themfelves work for repentance.

" Now you have done with your old partners, it is in your power to eftablifh your credit here, which will increafe your intereft and happinefs. I have acquired fuch a knowledge of your affairs, that I fee clearly how to gain you a glorious independance. It muft be by following the advice I have always given you, to purfue virtue, and nobly refufe to publifh all virulent pieces in your paper. Good men, of all denominations, would applaud you, and you would certainly pre- ferve the efteem and intereft of the FRIENDS, a peaceable people, whofe principles lead them to abhor all malice and rancour againft their fellow men, and they would not wink at it, even in the fuppofed author of the anonymous letter.———I am, with fervent wifhes for your fpiritual and temporal felicity, your affectionate mother,

SARAH GODDARD."

A friend of mine in *New-England* offered to be concerned with me, if he could purchafe *Towne's* right. We both fet out together, in *Sep- tember* laft, for this place, and, on our arrival, made a propofal to him, to give the fame that he had engaged to give, payable in the

the fame way, provided Meffrs. *Galloway* and *Wharton* would accept our bonds in the room of his.——Mr. *Towne*, after confulting his patrons, refufed, faying his fhare was worth £. 1000—but as I wanted to get him out of the office, he would fell for £. 526, in cafe he was left at liberty to fet up immediately, and take the government's bufinefs, which he faid he was fure Meffrs. *Galloway* and *Wharton* would give him, and what other bufinefs he could get, out of the office. This was fo unreafonable, that I advifed my friend not to trest any further with him; and after I had removed every difficulty that my enemies had thrown in my way, I fat off again, with my friend, to complete my bufinefs in *Providence*, &c. At this place I collected 600 dollars, which I devoted principally to the fupport of my bufinefs here, and actually fupplied it with every fheet of paper, and indeed every thing elfe ufed therein, and had lefs affiftance from my partner, than what I might have had from a common journeyman.

My bufinefs was a good deal interrupted, and the credit of the *Chronicle* leffened, thro' the low artifices of my partner. To prove this, I have a cloud of witneffes—But, thro' the indefatigable induftry and vigilance of my family, he was counteracted in his endeavours to get the whole bufinefs into his own hands. I had one book on which there were outftanding debts to the amount of near £. 2000. This he wanted to carry off. My fifter fufpecting his defign, from his behaviour, took particular care to carry it out of my compting-room, every night, and lock it up. This offended Mr. *Towne* fo much, that while fhe was directing the news papers to our country cuftomers, he fuddenly fnatched the lift from before her, which he detained, to the great injury of the bufinefs, till my return. This occafioned the papers to be very irregularly fent, as my fifter was obliged to make ufe of an old imperfect book that was accidentally preferved.

My friend, to whom I was indebted, not arriving, I could only bargain away my eftate, without being able to give a deed. I therefore, in *December*, fat out on my return home, and arrived at *New-York* about the firft of *January*, where I found a letter from my mother, of which the following is an extract, *viz.*

" I am fenfibly affected with all your unhappinefs. Your enemies have fpared no pains to ruin you —and grief has funk my fpirits, for your fake, by fuch a fcene of misfortunes, that I know not how to exprefs myfelf.——I can only hope, that you will bear up under them, not only like a man but like a chriftian, which would take off much of their weight, and give you more contentment than is ever to be found in ill-gotten wealth—Remember that true faying—' It is a more certain fign of a great mind to be a fufferings patiently, than to be a conqueror.' I can give you this confolation, however, that your *Chronicle* has daily new fubfcribers, and well conducted, would handfomely fupport two families. I fhall exert myfelf to preferve its credit, and with your affiftance it will revive and flourifh.——Sell your eftate, if poffible, if you let it go lower than the value, pay off Mr.——, and return, with all expedition, to your bufinefs.——I daily mourn for your hard fate, and while I live, which cannot be long, I fha'l be ftriving to promote your intereft here, as a proof of my affection

for you, and in return for the love and compaſſion you have mani-
feſted for your ancient and tender mother,

Philadelphia, Dec. 23, 1769. S. GODDARD."

The next day, after the receipt of the above, while I was antici-
pating the pleaſure of a happy ſight of my friends, I received the
following melancholy intelligence, of the death of my mother, from a
lady who is an ornament to her ſex, which happened *ſuddenly*, on
the fifth of *January :*

"' SIR,

" 'Tis with pain I take the pen to inform you (what your ſiſter has
not ſpirits to do) that your dear parent is no more. Your ſiſter
thinks it abſolutely neceſſary that you ſhould be here before the expiration of the third year of the *Chronicle*, as Mr. *Towne inſiſts on car-*
rying on a paper in his own name, which probably your being here
might prevent. She has, by adviſe of her friends, taken out a letter
of adminiſtration, to prevent any other perſons taking the affairs into
their hands. I adviſe you to come with all haſte. I have only time
to add, that I am yours, &c.

Jan. ———, 1770. ———————."

I ſet out immediately, with a heavy heart, and arrived to the infinite ſurpriſe and chagrin of Meſſrs. *Galloway, Wharton* and *Towne,*
who had given out that I could come here no more—that I owed large
ſums all over the world—that the *Chronicle* would ſoon appear in the
name of the latter—and that ' *every face in my houſe ſhould be changed.*'
Nothing could exceed their exultation on the pleaſing idea of the
expected revolution.

As ſoon as the unfortunate event of my mother's death took place,
my inhuman partner behaved in the moſt outrageous manner, ſwore
that he would print the paper in his own name, entered my houſe
where my mother lay a corpſe, and in a menacing manner inſulted
my ſiſter in her diſtreſs, ſwearing by G—d, that he wou'd have the
books. The company preſent expreſſed their horror and aſtoniſhment at ſuch unparalleled brutality—and adviſed my ſiſter, by no
means, to deliver the books to him, but to take out a letter of adminiſtration, and detain every thing in her hands till I arrived. This
ſhe punctually performed, with a ſpirit and addreſs that does her honour.

I muſt not here omit an anecdote, as a proof of Mr. *Galloway's*
generoſity, benevolence and goodneſs of heart. On the death of my mother, he paid my ſiſter a viſit ; and after condoling with her for the
great loſs ſhe had ſuſtained, for which he expreſſed the utmoſt concern, (though he and his colleague, by their injuſtice towards me,
had been a means of bringing her grey hairs with ſorrow to the grave)
he pulls a paper from his pocket, containing an eſtimate of the value
of my buſineſs, and by a *falſe view* of it, endeavoured to prevail on
my ſiſter to ſell it for a trifle ; for ſays he, " your brother will not, he
cannot return here—you have no friends here—you would live much
happier in *New-England*—and may make ſomething for yourſelf by
a ſale of this intereſt. You ſhall be paid annually a certain ſum to be
agreed on," My ſiſter ſaw his baſeneſs, and that he was a man who
could

could finile with a dagger in his hand, told him that fhe knew the bufinefs was very valuable, and that fhe fhould liften to no fuch propofals.. To this fhe generoufly added, that although by the fudden
death of my mother, one half of the intereft became hers, by law, yet
fhe would give it all up to me, as it was defigned for me. Mr. Galloway reprefented it a lofing bufinefs, and was fo kind as to with to take
it off my hands, to carry it on himfelf, to prevent my being a further
fufferer. I have it not in my power, on this occafion, to make him
a fuitable return for his benevolence; it muft therefore, like his other
virtue, be its own reward.——After all this kindnefs and generofity,
this jewel of a man, finding my fifter deaf to his council, came no
more to fhew his friendfhip and regard—but fet his tools and emiffa-
ries to work, to blaft my reputation, and ruin my intereft in this province.——This is Mr. Galloway, Gentlemen and Ladies!—How
do ye like him?

Upon a full difcovery of Mr. Towne's villainy, I judged it neceffary to infert an advertifement in the next Chronicle, that was publifhed after my return, that the public might know it, and to apolo-
gize for my abfence. This was fo oppofite to the intelligence he had
whifpered about, that he faid my apology was derogatory to his honour.
He therefore objected to its being printed in the Chronicle. I infert
a copy of it here, and appeal to the reader, whether there is the leaft
appearance of a defign to injure him. * My apprehenfions on account

* Philadelphia, Jan. 22, 1770.

☞ WILLIAM GODDARD, the eftablifher of the PENN-
SYLVANIA CHRONICLE, and UNIVERSAL AVERTISER, having car-
ried on the printing bufinefs for feveral years in a diftant province, and being
defirous to clofe his affairs there, in order to ferve his cuftomers here, more
to their and his own fatisfaction, hath been neceffarily detained from hence,
from time to time, for the greateft part of the year paft—and he hopes his
kind cuftomers will candidly confider this, and excufe any defects and inac-
curacies they may have obferved in this third volume, as well as the
want of that entertaining variety, which they might have expected from
his ingenious correfpondents, many of whofe favours have been omitted by
means of his abfence, and the indifpofition of a dear parent lately deceafed.
He begs leave to affure his cuftomers, and the public in general, that he is
now determined to attend his bufinefs in perfon, and to devote his whole
time and attention to their fervice, and, in a particular manner, to render
the CHRONICLE worthy of their further patronage and regard, by its
infertion of the moft valuable moral, hiftorical, political, and entertaining
pieces, and the frefheft and moft important intelligence from all quarters of
the globe.——He acknowledges, with a grateful heart, the many favours
he hath received from the public; and, in return, he intended to have made
confiderable improvements in his paper, agreeable to his late propofals; but
he has hitherto been prevented from giving that evidence of his gratitude,
by the non importation agreement of the merchants, it being impoffible to procure the neceffary articles from England, particularly paper, not but coun-
teracting the patriotic defigns of that refpectable body, which he hath care-
fully avoided, although he could have imported in a manner highly advan-
cive of his private intereft, without violating any of his own engagements.
The fame caufe now induces him to print the Chronicle on a fmaller paper
than ufual, (the fame fize, however, of the Gazette, Journal, &c.) for
fince

count of the expected suit, by the agent of my absent friend, were
not at an end; and thinking if I was arrested for such a large sum, at
that crisis, it might prove ruinous to me, I judged it prudent to make
overtures to the Gentleman, who made the demand upon me, before
I ran any risques. This was the only debt that ever put me in personal danger, and the case was attended with peculiar circumstances in
my favour.—My enemies had made themselves acquainted with this
affair, no doubt by means of my mother's and my own private letters,
which were intercepted and broken open, so that all my private affairs became known to those who were endeavouring to destroy my
fairest hopes in life, and gave them an opportunity to wound me, before I could put myself in a posture of defence. Two letters, one
from, and the other to, my mother, were accidentally found in Mr.
Towne's apartment, broken open, where he had concealed them for
months, in a repository of his own.——This was judged an excellent
opportunity to destroy me. The plan was fixed at once, and Mr.
Towne was to be the *traitor*. He therefore neglects finishing the
Chronicle, in order to bring me to the office; and the late publication he could, as he had often done, impute to me; and if I came to
finish it, as he expected, he could bring the sheriff upon me, and
the point would be settled; and he could take possession of the office,
in behalf of his masters, and fix their standard there. About 3 o'clock,
Monday afternoon, finding Mr. *Towne* absent, and the *Chronicle* not
published, I went into the office, and soon put it in a way of publication. In the mean time, Mr. *Towne* comes to the door, which was
fastened, in order to keep out the people, who were continually coming for the paper. Finding me there, he goes to the *German* church,
where the sheriff was attending a funeral. He there hung over the
pew door, in which the sheriff sat, till the solemn service was ended,
then followed him to the edge of the grave, and after the corpse
was deposited, this *perfidious man* whispered the sheriff in the ear—
" *Don't you want to see Mr.* Goddard? *I will, if you please, take you
to him!* The sheriff said he wanted to speak with me, on some business, and went with him to the office. Mr. *Towne* suddenly bursts
open

_since the agreement took place, he has been obliged to pay an extravagant
price for the large paper, at least nine shillings in a ream more than is given
by any other publisher of news-papers in this province, which is really to
heavy an expence for a paper at so small a price as ten shillings per annum.—This, he persuades himself, will be considered a sufficient apology
for the alteration, as well as for delaying the complete execution of his new
plan, till, by a repeal of the revenue acts, this country shall be relieved from
its present burthens.—He takes occasion at this time to mention, that by the
death of his mother, who had a share in the Chronicle, his sister, Mary
Catherine Goddard, is now interessed therein, in company with himself
and partner; and while he entreats a continuance of the public favour, in
behalf of the company, he earnestly requests all those who are indebted for
the Chronicle, advertisements, &c. to make immediate payment, which is
become absolutely necessary to enable him to settle a company concern, as
well as for the due prosecution of the business in future.—He flatters himself his benefactors, especially those in the country, and provinces adjacent,_
whom

burfts open the door and fays—" *There he is, Mr. Redman!* While this gentleman was going toward the fire, Mr. *Towne* fnatches up the form that I had been preparing, and which I had juft left, (to wait on a gentleman of my acquaintance, at my dwelling-houfe) and ran off with it. and, as I understand, put it in the poffeffion of the JUNTO, who lay on their arms all that night. My people thinking that Mr. *Towne* acted by legal authority did not oppofe him.——The fherif foon went home. My fifter waited on him, to know wherefore he took away my materials. He behaved with the humanity and politenefs of a chriftian and a gentleman, affured my fifter he had no hand in it, and laid open the treachery of my partner, declaring, if he knew where to find him, he would recover the form, if poffible. He feemed to entertain a proper idea of this unjuftifiable proceeding. My fifter then afked him, whether he had any demands upon me; he faid he had nothing but a bill of coft, which had occurred (by means of Mr. *Towne*, and his patrons) in my abfence.——This was immediately difcharged—And as my fifter was adminiftratrix to my mother's eftate, fhe thought proper to advertife the city of Mr. *Towne's* conduct. This alarmed the *fugitive* fo much, that he came to my fifter, and faid—" *For God's fake, fupprefs the advertifement, and I will bring back the form.—It has played the devil with me.*"—This was done, and the paper was publifhed.

I took an opportunity to tell him, that his behaviour was fuch, that nothing but a refpect to the memory of my mother, who was a lover of peace, prevented my chaftifing him as he deferved. His confcience dictating to him that he had acted a deteftable part, which was difcoverable in his very countenance, he then infifted on a *diffolution of the partnerfhip.* Pleafed with his *demand*, I told him if he would pay up his arrearages, and indemnify me from Meffrs. *Galloway* and *Wharton's* part of the company debts, I would do it directly, and would then give him what his fhare was really worth, if we could agree on terms of payment. But he would have the articles *firft deftroyed*, and *then* would fettle accounts!—I could not confent to fo prepofterous a mode of doing bufinefs, I therefore left him to follow the dictates of his matters' and his own *evil genius*, and went on with my bufinefs, as if there was no fuch man as Mr. *Towne* upon earth. He, however foon called my attention to him; for, *by favour of the night*, he carried off another *form*, in order to force a compliance with *his mode* of fettlement. I had now got a fufpenfion of the expected procefs againft me, till the arrival of my friend from abroad, fo that I could, without fear, hunt the *fugitive*. I foon found him, concealed in a *garret*, and upon my reprefenting to him the impropriety of his behaviour, and the danger of a profecution or a *broken head*, added to the advice of feveral gentlemen, who declared that my propofals were fair and equitable, and that he would injure himfelf, he delivered it up. Determined he fhould

G   not

<hr>

whom he has it not in his power to wait upon perfonally, will readily comply with his requeft, by getting fome of their friends, or the merchants they deal with, to pay off their accounts, which tho' but fmall, yet, by being all collected together, will be of great fervice to himfelf, as well as to the perfons with whom he is connected in bufinefs.

not ferve me fuch a trick a third time, I fix'd a proper trap for him—but he efcaped it by altering his plan of operations. His next attempt was more difhonourable than the laft. Being arrefted for a fum of money, he offers his creditor a bond and judgment, payable in one week, or one day, provided he would attach my printing-office as his property, and let his perfon be fafe. This he judged was an effectual way to harrafs me, as I fhould be obliged to enter into a lawfuit, or have my bufinefs ftopped. But this creditor, being a man of honour, and poffeft of the *feelings* of *humanity*, told him that he would *lofe the whole debt*. before he would be guilty of fo vile an action. He was about doing the fame to another—and actually gave a bond, and bill of fale of one half of the materials to the gentleman whom he had engaged to pay the £. 40, mentioned in p. 41. He even brought the gentleman into the office to take poffeffion of them, that they might be taken out of my hands, advertifed and fold, to the ruin of my credit and bufinefs. I then was obliged to ufe all the art in my power. I acquainted the gentleman that there was nothing in my houfe at Mr. *Towne*'s difpofal, and that I would convince him of it if he would call upon me another time. If he had any intereft in company with me, there was no known criterion to diftinguifh his particular part, and it would be unjuft, to the laft degree, to take and fell my types, to get at what was conveyed to him by Mr. *Towne*. for a malicious wicked purpofe. My office being detached from my place of abode, and fubject, in my abfence, to the inroads of my enemies, I was advifed, on this occafion, immediately to take all the printing materials under my own roof, where I could go on without interruption. This I did at noon-day, before the face of my daftardly partner, who trembled like an afpin leaf ; run about, from fquare to fquare, making a heavy complaint ; and indeed gave every alarm in his power, except ringing the fire bell. I coolly gave him the reafons of my conduct, and that tho' I was determined no longer to fubmit to his interruptions ; yet, if he had a *ftomach to his work*, which he had loft fome time before, under an idea that it was a difgrace for a mafter-printer to work, he fhould have egrefs and regrefs. and all the advantage of the books that an *honeft man* could defire ; but that I would not fuffer them to be taken out of the office, on any pretence whatever.——

Poor *Towne* was now in great perplexity. His guilt and his pride would not permit him to accept of my offer. He therefore entirely abandons the printing-office, and has ever fince, above fix months, been employed in picking up, by *deceit* and *collufion*, fmall fums of money due to me here and there, for which he renders no account, and in defaming my character. His malice carried him to the houfes of almoft every perfon with whom I had dealings, in order to induce them to fue me for whatever fums I might owe. He fucceeded but with one ignorant man ; the reft defpifed him ; told him that they knew him not ; that they never fhould have thought of afking him for any part of my debts, and that they doubted not but I would pay them with honour.

The 19th of *May*, agreeable to the articles, Mr. *Towne* had a
right

right to demand a settlement of accounts. I prepared myself for him; but he did not make his appearance. About the last of this month, my friend, to whom I was indebted for my materials, gave me notice of his arrival. In consequence of which, I went to *New-England*, sold my estate, and paid him to his satisfaction ; who, on hearing of the treatment I had met with, and the unlucky circumstances which had occurred, generously returned part of the money, to enable me to preserve myself from the persecution of my enemies.

Upon my return, I found my enemies had not been idle. A worthless man, to whom I owed *forty shillings* for labour, was, by *some means*, INDUCED to swear on the Holy Evangelists of Almighty God that I had gone off to defraud my creditors, and to bring in an account for *ten pounds* against me, whereby he got out a domestic attachment, in order to call in all to whom I was indebted, and effect my ruin. A gentleman of credit in this city, discovered the plot, and gave notice to my sister, who instantly sent the money to the sheriff—and on my return, I waited on him, produced a true state of the case, and the man was obliged to settle with me agreeable thereto, so that I received the greatest part of the money again. This poor wretch, who took the oath, was soon thrown into gaol, and my resentment is changed into pity and compassion for his doubly unhappy condition.

As Mr. *Towne* neglected to call upon me for the settlement of accounts, some time in *June*, I applied to him for that purpose. He knew he was confiderably in arrear to me, and apprehended that I should sue him and throw him into gaol, as he actually told me. To be before-hand with me, he gets out a writ against me, which was served upon me while I was requesting him to settle accounts. I was held to bail in the sum of £. 500, on a plea that I hold the covenants, &c. with him made. Sensible that this was a stratagem of *Galloway* and *Wharton*, to save their £. 526, which they have entirely lost, in my opinion, by their endeavours to ruin me, I was under no concern, but went away and gave bail ; and I am persuaded whenever it is tried by a jury, which I intend it shall be, that I may have the satisfaction of confronting Messrs. *Galloway*, *Wharton* and *Towne*, before the public, I shall have it in my power to prove, by undeniable testimony, the injuries I have received ; and I doubt not but I shall obtain such a verdict as will reflect no dishonour upon *my* reputation.

My enemies finding that I could get bail for so large a sum, were much surprised. What step to take next they were at a loss. They concluded, at last, to endeavour to alarm the fears of my customers, by a publication that should, by implication, affect my credit, so that, by that means, my customers would not pay me for the *Chronicle*, &c. and my finances would be exhausted, and I should *at last* fall a prey to them. In consequence of this, an advertisement appears in the *Pennsylvania Journal* of the 12th of *July* last, which laid me under the disagreeable necessity to reply, in order to prevent unfavourable impressions on the minds of my friends and customers. These advertisements I think proper to insert here, in order to lay open the whole process.

Frow.

From the *Pennsylvania Journal*, of *July* 12, 1770.

WHEREAS, a partnership was some time ago entered into between *William Goddard* and *Benjamin Towne*, which, on experiment, is found to be inconvenient, I, the said *Benjamin Towne*, do therefore for legal as well as expedient confiderations decline the connexion, and defire that no perfon in future will rely on my credit as a partner in their contracts and dealings with the faid *William Goddard*.

And whereas a perfon is appointed, on behalf of the principal creditors of the prefs to receive fo much of the fubfcription money due from the inhabitants of the city and diftricts for the *Chronicle*, as will difcharge his debt, the faid *Benjamin Towne* therefore can only defire the fubfcribers for the faid paper, in other places, to pay their fubfcription money to him (at Mrs. *Ma* ſt's in Second-ftreet, near Chrift-Church) as he has been a confiderable fufferer by the partnerſhip, and only wiſhes to have the company's debts paid.   BENJAMIN TOWNE.

From the *Pennfylvania Journal*, of *July* 26, 1770.

Philadelphia, *July* 21, 1770.

IT has been my great misfortune to be concerned in bufinefs, for fome time paft, with a very unworthy man under the name of *Benjamin Towne*, formerly a journeyman in my office, a perfon very little known here, till he was drawn from obfcurity to be made the fcape-goat of his fuperiors, to bear off their iniquity.

Had I not fatally experienced in him a total want of that honour and veracity, which alone can diftinguifh the good man from the villain, the man of merit from the undeferving, I fhould really be aftonifhed at the matchlefs effrontery of the foregoing advertifement; but when I confider his repeated bafe violation of his word and honour, his continually divulging the important fecrets of my bufinefs to two party men, who would facrifice even their native country, to gratify an enormous luft of power, under whofe banners he has inlifted himfelf; his attempt to defraud an antient gentlewoman, his brutality and ungentlemanlike behaviour in my family, and the vile calumnies he has propagated againſt me, in low malignant whifpers, added to that flagrant breach of truft, the opening and fuppreffing private letters entrufted to his care, my furprife is wholly abforbed in the indignation I feel for fuch fuperlative proftitution, fuch an entire departure from thofe facred laws of honour and juftice, which are the ftrongeft bands of civil fociety.——Notwithftanding I have now a fair opportunity of fhewing the world the cruel treatment I have met with from Mr. *Towne*, and his two patrons, yet as our difpute is of fuch a nature, as muft ere long bring it before a court of judicature, where I flatter myfelf I fhall be allowed a fair and candid hearing, and have an opportunity to lay open all the fecret villainy that hath been practifed towards me, from the violating private letters to the writing and circulating others without fignature, to murder my reputation, I am not difpofed to enter into a paper war with Mr. *Towne*; for I do not think it juft to endeavour to anticipate the judgment of thofe before whom the cafe may come in a judicial way, by premature publications—and my fole aim, on this occafion, is, to fhew the folly and extreme malice of Mr. *Towne's* prefent advertifement. Befides, were it neceffary to lay a complete ftate of the cafe before the public, I fhould only confider Mr. *Towne* as the *Jackall* to other animals, who are now lying perdue to feize on me their devoted prey. The whole, however, will hereafter appear, even if I were fure *Jack Retort*, *Lex Talionis*, *Americanus*, and the whole pack fhould be let loofe upon me.

After this infatuated man had in vain exerted himfelf to deftroy my bufnefs, that he might rife on its ruin, by ufing a variety of low deteftible
artifices,

(53)

artifices, to interrupt and defeat the industry of my family, particularly in stopping the regular publication of the *Chronicle*, by carrying off, under cover of the night, the forms as they stood composed and corrected for the press, as also the lists of the customers, &c. which last he *heroically* snatched from the hands of my sister, and *ran* off with them; and finding himself stopt in his career, in such a manner, that he had not spirit and resolution to withstand, with chagrin and despair he abandoned the office in *February* last; ever since which, he has concealed his lodgings so effectually, that even the TAX-GATHERERS have not been able to find out his retreat.— He has indeed frequently made *excursions* abroad; and because I would not permit him to overthrow the business, by carrying off the books, for the emolument of himself and —— and ——, (who have *over-reached* themselves in their negotiations with him) he tells a *lamentable tale*, which sounds harsh to those who are ignorant of the true state of matters, *that he has been arbitrarily deprived of his* PROPERTY—when it is an indubitable truth, that he has never been denied the free use of the books, &c. where they ought to be used, and where there was any safety in entrusting them into his hands. The propriety of this caution will further appear, when it is considered, that the late Mrs. *Goddard's* interest would have greatly suffered by a loss of the books and papers, she having joined in a bond with Mr. *Towne*, with a view of serving him as well as me, for the payment of a considerable sum of money, without having any consideration, or any other security than the possession of the books, &c. which, on her death, fell, of course, into the hands of her heirs, who are determined to discharge *her* contracts, as well as *their own*, in the most honourable manner, of which all persons concerned may have a satisfactory assurance, on an application at my house.

It is a fact indisputable, that when Mr. *Towne* joined me, he had not a single shilling, but what he drew from my pocket—that he paid nothing to those whose right he bought, it being stipulated, that they should receive their pay from him in printing work, which they were to furnish—that he has not, during our connexion, advanced *Thirty Pounds* towards the support of the house, or provided it with a single sheet of paper, or any other kind of stock; and it is by no means probable that his *credit* could procure any, when he had no other recource for subsistence money but the Printing Office—and that I have borne the weight of almost all the company debts—without any real aid from him or those men, who, by a mean subterfuge, threw *their debts* on my shoulders.

There is an absurd ambiguity in the advertisement in question, when, if the author had been actuated by justice, he might have spoken boldly out. It however, in a manner, discovers that the design was only to lessen my credit amongst my customers—It has somewhere been justly observed, that in such performances, where scandal was the object, "dark phrases are to be studied, and a confused description will be frequent, with a perplexity of expression, between saying what the writer's rancour will not let him withhold, and withholding what his fear will not let him speak out." I think it necessary to explain it. Mr. *Towne* found himself detected and defeated in his base manœuvres to avail himself of my absence in a distant province, and an unfortunate event in my family, to get the whole business, that I had, at a very great expence, established, into his own hands, therefore *very justly* observes, that the partnership "has been found, on EXPERIMENT, very *inconvenient*"—when it would most assuredly have been very *convenient* to any honest industrious man. To shew his *wonderful sagacity*, he adds, "*I therefore decline the connexion*"—as if a man, under articles of agreement, could at any time violate them from motives of *conveniency*. He then modestly desires no-

body

body to " rely on *his credit* as a partner, in their contracts and dealings
with me." It is to be lamented that any man will take so much pains
to make himself contemptible, for the small gratification of being considered *one week* a man of consequence. Had he dispassionately considered
his own real situation, he must have known that all his boasted credit
could only exist till the periodical return of the next *Journal* or *Gazette*:
For I can, at any time, make it appear, that this vain boaster is now in
arrear to me nearly to the amount of £. 200—and that he has now no
other support than the picking up small sums of money, due to the
company——for which he gives no credit; except he now and then receives a *decent*, which I believe to be small enough, from the *bene-
volent* and *upright* DUUMVIRATE. I can safely say, I never asked for
or received any credit on this man's account, or entertained an idea of
such a thing—as I while I heartily second his request, that nobody would
rely on *his credit*, &c. I congratulate him on his apparent safety. For my
part, I only desire to be equally safe with regard to him.

His assertion, that " a person is appointed by the *principal Creditors*†
of the press to receive so much of the subscription money due from the
inhabitants of the city and districts, for the *Chronicle*, as will discharge
his debt," I do hereby solemnly declare to be an *absolute falsehood*, which
I stand ready to make appear. As to his request to the subscribers " *in
other places*", to pay *him*, it is too ridiculous to deserve notice; for I am
confident no man of common discernment would pay money to a FUGI-
TIVE, who holds no ties of honour or contracts binding, but such as are
convenient to his own purposes, and who has not a book or account,
whereby he could ascertain a debt, or give the proper credit. The books,
&c. are in my possession, and whenever my customers, (a continuance of
whose favours I earnestly request) find it convenient to pay for the paper,
I should be glad they would call upon me for that purpose, when they
shall have credit on the books, and proper receipts.

Upon the whole, though Mr. *Towne* is not entitled to my esteem and
confidence, yet he has a right to justice, and he shall have it to all intents
and purposes; and I now call upon him to *appear*, and settle his accounts,
agreeable to the articles, and if he cannot pay his arrearages, I will take
the security of his patrons—for I should be rejoiced when I can be " *le-
gally*" relieved from the dishonour and slavery of such a connexion; upon
which happy event, I shall not forget my promises to the Public, of im-
proving the *Chronicle*, in return for the indulgence and favour they have
shewn their grateful obliged humble servant,

WILLIAM GODDARD.

Soon after the appearance of my advertisement, Mr. *Galloway* sent
in the following account, and demanded payment, with a threat to
sue me if I did not comply.——As I never had any dealings with
Mr.

---

† *Upon the first appearance of Mr.* Towne's *advertisement, he was
charged with the falshood of this assertion, by a person well acquainted with
our affairs. Alarmed at this sudden detection, he flies to the printer, and
gets an alteration made, whereby he hopes to obviate the charge of falshood
in this particular instance, by reducing it to a malicious misrepresentation
and imposture—for which I am willing he should have due credit.—From
the extraordinary movements of the junto, at this warm season of the year,
and the borrowing and lending dictionaries, and the humble attempt at
journalry, it is given out, that they are manufacturing a piece that will
outdo their usual outdoings; therefore I think proper to reserve myself for
the stating this matter, &c. till I see their performance.——It is said Mr.
G—— is its father it.*

Mr. *Strahan*, and my partnerſhip with *Towne* muſt have been unknown to him, and he was Mr. *Galloway*'s correſpondent, I query
whether or no this account was not *manufactured* by Mr. *Galloway*,
in his own office, from the one Mr. *Strahan* ſent him, wherein he was
himſelf made debtor.

Dr. WILLIAM GODDARD and BENJAMIN TOWNE,
To WILLIAM STRAHAN, Cr.

April 16, 1768. Paid for *Chronicles*, as per receipts, £.	3	15	6
For *Chronicles* from *January* 5, 1768, to *January* 5, 1770, as per receipts from the poſt office,	8	8	0
To *London Chronicles*, from *February* 23, 1767, to *January* 1, 1770, ſent by Mr. *Nichell*,	8	18	6
To *Lloyd*'s do. from do. to do.	8	18	6
To 2 *Gent. Mag.* from do. to do.	1	18	0
To 2 *London* do. from do. to do.	1	18	0
To 2 *Univ. Mag.* from do. to do.	1	18	0
Coffee-houſe charges with the above,	3	5	0

£. 38 : 17 : 6

I ſent a lad to Mr. *Galloway*, with a written meſſage, that *I ſhould
be glad to converſe with him on buſineſs.* He ſaid he would not—he
had *no buſineſs with me.* I then ſent to know, as he had ' *no buſineſs
with me,*' why he ſent in an account againſt me. He ſaid he had paid
the money in *England,* and would be repaid. I gave myſelf no further trouble about the matter, and am determined never to pay a farthing of it, until Meſſrs. *Galloway* and *Wharton* ſtep forth and diſcharge their debts, when I ſhall willingly pay one half of that account.

My advertiſement, I underſtand, ſo galled the JUNTO, that an
extraordinary council was called, at the *theatre of ſcandal,* where,
after ſome debate, it was VOTED and RESOLVED, that a ſecond
" *humble attempt at ſcurrility*" ſhould be made, as nothing had ever
ſerved their purpoſe ſo well as the firſt. Each one was to make an
eſſay, and produce his performance at the next meeting. This, it is
ſaid, was done ; but alas ! when they convened again, and each man's
labours had been read, it was impoſſible to connect or *bind* their ſcan-
dalous anecdotes together, without uſing ſuch a number of the
WITHS, that their *favorite author,* JACK RETORT, mentions, as would
make their work look *bungling.* After ſome inteſtine broils, each one
being tenacious of his own performance, it was judged moſt for the
advantage of the *common cauſe,* to burn this farrago of nonſenſe and
ſcurrility, and appoint a ſelect committee to draw up another ; which
being done, accordingly, an advertiſement appears, after a while, ad-
dreſſed to the Public, more particularly to the kind cuſtomers of the
Pennſylvania Chronicle, &c. printed in hand-bills, and afterwards inſerted in the *Pennſylvania Journal,* under the name of *Benjamin
Towne,* in which my enemies have ſet no boundaries to their malice—
They

They have not only sported with my calamities, in the most inhuman manner, and given the most invidious turn to every thing that has occurred—but invented abundance of the most abominable and malicious falshoods—ABSOLUTE FALSEHOODS, WITHOUT THE LEAST FOUNDATION IN TRUTH. In the language of a worthy writer, I ask, —What punishment is severe enough to inflict on that wretch, who in violation of every law of society, in despite of honour, truth, and justice, sacrifices all mankind to the licentious scandal of his tongue and pen, and at every blast of his foul breath, and every dash of his pen, would make a reputation die?

My business requiring my almost constant personal attendance, I cannot follow them thro' all their meanders of scurrility, nor do strict justice to their characters, by unfolding to the world every instance of their injustice; yet a regard to my own reputation, impels me to make some few observations upon this performance which has been ushered into the world under the name of *Benjamin Towne*, tho' I hope I have said enough already to invalidate every thing he has said against me.

He sets out with a *foolish* charge against me and calls upon me to *defend* myself, that I am of a *hot* and *combustible temper* and a *choleric. disposition*. He might, with equal propriety, have called me to the bar of the public for having a *longer nose* than he has. I should, in such a case, be obliged to plead *guilty*; but I should undoubtedly obtain the favour of the court, if I could prove, as I think I can, that I refused to follow the example of my accuser, of being LED BY THE NOSE. It is not a man's warmth of disposition, that renders him by any means criminal, and accountable to the public, but for acts of imprudence arising therefrom; and I am confident Mr. *Towne* cannot shew any such act, that can possibly entitle me to such a character, unless detecting fraud, and holding the authors (no better than pickpockets) up to view, and chastising insolence, injustice and brutality, will fix it upon me. In such a view of the matter, I don't know but I may be a little *combustible* and *choleric*; and I believe the most rigid devotee upon earth, situated as I have been, would have shewn some warmth of temper, and been a little *choleric* too, as Mr. *Towne* is made to express himself——and whenever a villain attempts my honour or purse, I believe I shall always shew that I am made of such *materials* as will TAKE FIRE, and shall think it no disgrace if Mr. *Towne*, or his masters, cry out, that I am. *combustible* and *choleric*. Such a character, however, as Mr. *Towne* means to give me, is entirely repugnant to my natural disposition, which is well known to a numerous and respectable acquaintance in several provinces, particularly in *N. York*, *Rhode-Island*, and *Connecticut*, to the two former of which I have been importuned to return, and set up my business. The following letter, signed by the Honourable DANIEL JENCKES, and JOHN COLE, Esqrs, with other gentlemen of reputation in *Providence*, urging my return to that place, where I have lived with the greatest satisfaction, will shew that they think differently of me there: and I hope my publishing it here will not be thought vain or impertinent.

" SIR,

" Sir,

" The particular efteem and friendfhip which we have for you, makes us regret your abfence: but when we confider the lofs of you as a printer, we cannot but expoftulate with you on that fubject.

" We have been, and ftill are of opinion, that this town, regarding it in its fituation, and the various lights in which a man of bufinefs might view it, would afford a very comfortable profpect to a young man of your occupation, in his fettlement among us.

" You may be affured, that from the knowledge we have of your expertnefs in the printing-bufinefs, we fhould prefer you, as our printer, to any other perfon ; excluſive of the other favourable impreffions you have made upon us, during the courfe of your refidence here.

" We very much deplore the difcontinuance of a public paper, in this town, efpecially at a time when that machine is become neceffary for the retention of our rights, by explaining to the people the nature of them, and founding an alarm when they are in danger.— We make no doubt but a fuitable number of good fubfcribers might be procured, and no prefs in America could more eafily be furnifhed with ftock, as the paper-mill is got to work.

" In this fituation of the town, with refpect to the printing-bufinefs, we fhould be much obliged to you for a declaration of your intent, in regard to the reviving your bufinefs here, to the end, that if you fhould altogether decline it (which we hope will not be the cafe) we might be free to make application to fome other printer, which, in fuch cafe, we fhall do in juftice to ourfelves.

" The foregoing letter is agreeable to the fentiments of all the gentlemen of the town, with whom we have converfed on the fubject, although figned only by Sir,
Your moft obedient and moft humble fervants,
Daniel Jenckes, John Cole, S. Downer, Nathan Angell, John Updike, Nicholas Brown, Hayward Smith, Ebenezer Thompfon, John Jenckes, James Angell, Mofes Brown, Job Smith, Jonathan Ballou, Jofeph Lawrence, John Nafh, James Arnold, John Brown, Jofeph Brown, Samuel Nightingale, jun. Jofeph Ruffel."

" Mr. William Goddard."

Mr. *Towne* fays, no motive could have induced him to publifh his libel, but that of juftifying *his character*. The fallacy of this muft be evident, as he flides over the criminal charges I brought againft him, and begins to recriminate upon me ; as if his alledging any thing to my difadvantage, could juftify him for a violation of the laws of honour, juftice, and humanity.

His affertions and infinuations that I owed him £. 65 : 7 : 5 ; that he was importuned to join me ; that he made the leaft objection thereto on any account whatever ; that he became bound for me ; or that he advanced or contributed any thing, by credit, or otherwife, in any fhape whatever, for my relief or benefit, I do hereby folemnly declare to be *abfolute falfhoods*. On the contrary—he was crouded upon me by the perfecution of Meffrs. *Galloway* and *Wharton*, who wanted a reprefentative of themfelves, or a proper tool to ferve their purpofes, that he came in with the *utmoft* eagernefs, obferving at the

H   time

time that I had always treated him in the politeſt manner, and that he did not doubt but we ſhould agree; that he never put in any ſtock, but deceived me with a plauſible ſtory, that he ſhould ſoon put in his types, and £ 300 in caſh, which proved an impoſition, and that he never advanced twenty ſhillings (I once ſaid thirty pounds) that I believe he could juſtly call his own, for the proſecution of the buſineſs, as I continually diſcover his receiving money, and giving his receipts under the firm of *Goddard* and *Towne*, of which he gives no account, that I may give the proper credit in the books.

With regard to the regular publication of the *Chronicle*, in my abſence or preſence, I never was indebted to the induſtry, capacity, or fidelity of Mr. *Towne*, tho' he claims the merit of it, for his *genius* was unequal to the management of any great concern; and after he became my partner, and I diſcovered his principles and connexions, I never placed any confidence in him, but always left my directions with a man of greater ability, to whoſe fidelity and zeal for my intereſt, added to the aſſiſtance of other faithful people, I am indebted for the regular publication of the *Chronicle*, amidſt the difficulties thrown in the way by Mr. *Towne* and his matters. He ſays that the *Chronicle* ſeldom came out till *Tueſday*, before he became a partner. If this was true, as it is not, there having never been but one inſtance of its being publiſhed on *Tueſday*, and that aroſe from an extraordinary occurrence, it muſt reflect great diſcredit upon him, as he was then a journeyman, employed on the *Chronicle*, at near £ 90 per annum; tho' I now think it was rather a penſion, on my eſtabliſhment, fixed upon him by *Galloway* and *Wharton*, for *ſecret ſervices*. By his own account he was a *poor ſervant*; and he has never yet given a clear evidence of his being a *better maſter*.

Having given the public, in the preceding part of this hiſtory, a faithful account of the ſituation of my affairs, and the inhuman conduct of my partners, by which they can eaſily form a true judgment of the motives of their conduct, as well as the occaſion of my ſeveral journies and long abſence abroad, and the principles I acted upon, I paſs over the mean unmanly inſinuations of Mr. *Towne*, of my being obliged to keep houſe; that I retreated from my buſineſs and creditors, and left my affairs on *his ſhoulders*; that I acted an underhanded part; that I violated my engagements; that I wanted to blaſt *his character*, and all the *police* epithets of villain, profligate calumniator, &c. &c. which he has beſtowed upon me, " *with the contempt they deſerve*," as the falſhood, miſrepreſentation, injuſtice and improbability of the whole muſt evidently appear, on a candid peruſal of the foregoing ſtate of facts, which can, in general, be eaſily proved by the teſtimonies of creditable witneſſes, or many corroborating circumſtances.

Mr. *Towne* aſſerts, that I tampered with him to become a party concerned in a fraudulent commerce, by urging him to purchaſe, upon credit, a quantity of paper of one paper-maker, in order that I might take it to *New-York*, and ſell it for ready money, to pay another to whom we owed money, and who was importunate, and that he *virtuouſly* refuſed, as it was robbing *Peter* to pay *Paul*. This is
a high,

a high charge ; I therefore beg leave to flate the matter in its true light, and I will abide by the confequences. The very day I received Mr. *Towne* into company with me, in the room of Meffrs. *Galloway* and *Wharton*, he *generoufly* propofed drinking a pot of beer with me ; whereupon I told him if he would flep to my houfe, or the *Golden Fleece*, I would give him a bottle of claret. He chofe the latter. Over this bottle, I gave him a fhort detail of all the advantages of the bufinefs, and particularly mentioned that I had made money by purchafing large quantities of paper at the mills, and fending it abroad for fale at an advanced price —I had made a practice of fhipping paper, in this manner, ever fince my arrival here, to *Jamaica, Carolina, Newport, Providence,* and *New-York.* I further told him that I had then an order from *New-York* for a quantity, that I thought it would be a good fcheme to purfue the trade, as others did, and if he pleafed he might be concerned with me. He replied, "'Tis an excellent fcheme. Have I not made a good day's work, to buy for £. 526, what is worth £. 1000?" I told him he had, if Meffrs. *Galloway* and *Wharton* would perform their promifes. I was led to mention the affair of paper, on account of his telling me he could command £. 300 ; and I told him that if he advanced at any time more money than me, I would affift him in paying his debt to Meffrs. *Galloway* and *Wharton*. Confidering where this converfation happened, and the fituation in which I left my new partner, I do not wonder he forgot himfelf.—I went to *Maryland*, as I have already related, a few days after, and when I returned, and difcovered his behaviour refpecting the power of attorney, I broke off all correfpondence with him, fcarcely exchanging a word with him ; therefore this propofal could not have been made at any other time than I have mentioned—Befides, we dealt with no other paper-maker, who could be importunate, but Mr. *Hazey,* and we fettled all matters to *his fatisfaction* when we joined, otherwife I would never have fubmitted to fuch a meafure. Moreover I purchafed the very paper I afked Mr. *Towne* to be concerned in, of Mr. *Hazey,* with the fame opennefs and fairnefs of dealing every man ought to purfue; and after I had it in my houfe many weeks, I fold it to a gentleman at *New York.* and paid for it when it fuited by conveniency, which will appear by the following extract of a letter from Mrs. *Goddard,* dated *July* —, 1769, received at *New-York,* on my way to *Rhode-Ifland.*

" This day I have fhipt on board Captain *Ferguſon* fifty-two reams of paper, agreeable to Mr. *Holt's* orders, for which I have paid Mr. *Hazey* all the cafh, except about *Forty Shillings.*"

I appeal, ' with the confcious pride of virtue,' to all the merchants in this province, if this is a ' fraudulent commerce,' or whether I am, by the moft forced conftruction, culpable, for carrying on fuch a trade as I have mentioned ; and no other did I ever attempt or think of. But fince recrimination is become a fafhionable mode of defence, I have a good opportunity to do it here.

When Mr. *Towne* was about to give a bond to Meffrs. *Galloway* and *Wharton* for £. 526 *cafh,* payable in one year, I told the latter, that I thought it would be beft for Mr. *Towne* to give an obligation

Io,

for the money payable in five yearly payments, £. 100 in each, as it was impossible for him to pay all that money in one year, in printing work, and advance his part of the expences of the office ; that the government's business, wou'd annually pay about the sum I mentioned ; and that if Mr. *Towne* furnished what he promised, I would give up my share of the profits arising from that business, to enable him to pay off his debt to him and Mr. *Galloway.*——Mr. *Wharton* then told me (and *Galloway* had signified something similar when we laid the foundation of our *amicable settlement*) that they had an easy way to get their money, and I need not be concerned for " *friend Towne.*" They intended to obtain a grant of the Assembly for £. 1000, for reprinting the body of laws, that thereby ' *friend Galloway*' would get a good job in revising, &c. and we a valuable one in printing, and they should get their whole debt *in a lump*, and the residue should be appropriated to the purchase of paper, and other expences of the work, which we might do at our leisure. This would *not* be robbing *Peter* to pay *Paul*, as Man *Towne* is made *wittily* to say ; but it will no doubt be thought that it would be robbing the Public to pay Tom and Joe.

The account Mr. *Towne* has given of his conferences with me, and the conversation that arose on these occasions, is an entire departure from the truth. Nothing of the kind he mentions ever happened. As to his other high charge, that I sold him printing materials, which I declared were my mother's, and that I endeavour now to prove so to his prejudice, is a very barefaced falshood, which must render him very contemptible in the eyes of every honest man ; for notwithstanding he endeavours to make the public believe that he purchased materials of me, I solemnly declare, and can fully prove, that I never sold him any thing of the kind. His purchase was of Messrs. *Galloway* and *Wharton*, which he and they want to *conceal*, to whom he gave security for himself, and not for me, which I can demonstrate, if I have not already done it, by their own hand writing : And the security I gave my mother, which Mr. *Towne* was well acquainted with before he joined me, it being done before numbers of people in the most open manner, could not possibly affect any property that was not my own, as can be easily discovered by the least attention to the instrument signed by my mother and me, inserted in No. I, p. 26--27. He does not pretend to charge Mrs. *Goddard* with any design to defraud him, yet it is impossible to separate us in that transaction ; for she not only signed the instrument with me, but was a witness to my articles of agreement with him, interested herself in setting aside the *old partnership*, and forming the *new one.* Besides, it was put on record, in a fair way, which was not absolutely necessary. Had I really done any thing that would not stand the test of a critical examination, is it probable that I (with so much artifice and presence of mind as my accuser gives me) should put myself into the power of a man I wou'd not trust with a single shilling, nor do any business with, if I could possibly help it ; and one who I knew would take any advantage of me that should fall in his way ? It must appear very strange if there was any the least foundation for his charge, that he should remain so long silent on fo extraordinary a cafe. Why did he not complain to Mrs. *God-dard* about it? He made the difcovery, he fays, by my *own information*, in *October* laft, THREE MONTHS before her death, yet he never fays a fingle fyllable about it till *July* —, 1770, then, being reduced to his *laft fhift*, becomes defperate in the difhonourable fervice he is in, and difperfes his calumnies, or rather thofe of his patrons, at random, like fire-brands, arrows and death. After all, I am ready to make it appear, either in or out of court, that I have not deprived Mr. *Towne* of any property of his, nor done any thing inconfiftent with law or equity—And I defy even that *law-learned penetrating* and *incomprehenfible* GENIUS *Galloway*, to fix any thing difhonourable upon me, if he pays the leaft regard to truth.

Mr. *Towne*'s laft charge that I clandeftinely appointed a perfon to collect the debts of the partnerfhip, to the detriment not only of himfelf, but the creditors of the company, is the greateft perverfion of truth ever attempted to be impofed upon mankind. I ever collected the outftanding debts of the company, and gave credit in the moft upright manner, as will appear by the books in my hands. It is true I did employ a man of honour to affift my mother, who could not go abroad, in my abfence, becaufe Mr. *Towne* was not to be trufted, and this gentleman executed the truft to my fatisfaction, notwithftanding all the obftacles Mr. *Towne* threw in his way; and when he had done, he delivered up thofe accounts that he could not get difcharged, with the money he had collected, to my filler, who entered it in the books, Mr. *Towne* being incapable of making a proper entry; and fhe appropriated the cafh to the difcharge of thofe company debts that were unjuftly thrown upon me. His reflection on the gentleman employed in this fervice, who is now abfent, is bafe and cowardly, and his fulfome compliment afterwards, is mean and contemptible: And I am very certain, the firft time he fees Mr. *Towne*, he will pay him a compliment in return. He has a proper knowledge of his treachery, and has cautioned me to beware of him. This Mr. *Towne* may have under his own hand, if he pleafes.

His infinuations that he could relate feveral facts of the *blackeft dye* againft me, but that he draws a veil over them from motives of humanity, is ridiculous to the laft degree. He might as well have faid that I had committed murder, and that he, from pure *good-will* to me, concealed it from the world. Can it be imagined that this man, after the *tendernefs* he has already manifefted, and the *regard* he has fhewn for my *intereft* and *reputation*, would publifh the lefs criminal matters firft, when he might, by proving one crime of the '*blackeft dye*,' completely effect his defign—my ruin. Mr. *Towne* and his matters are fenfible how much pain the leaft imputation of difhonour ever gave me, they therefore know how to wound me, and they will not fail to exert themfelves. I cannot prevent a villainous charge; but I defy the moft malignant of all the human race, whom I believe to be this TRIUMVIRATE, to prove any thing derogatory to my honour as a gentleman, except my connecting myfelf with them, which, however, I hope will rather be confidered a misfortune than a fault: And I now call upon them to ftep forth, fhew

their

their faces in public, and confront me for that purpose, or take to themselves the infamy of having imposed upon the public, in the most dastardly manner.

> "————————All your attempts
> Shall fall on me like brittle shafts on armour
> That break themselves; or like waves against a rock
> That leave no sign of their o'erboiling fury
> But foam and splinters: My innocence, like those,
> Shall stand triumphant."————

The behaviour of Mr. *Towne*, on the death of Mrs. *Goddard*, I have related without any exaggeration; yet he endeavours artfully to smooth over his conduct on that occasion, and tries to make it appear as if my sister had united with me in a plan to defraud him and the creditors of the company. But her conduct in exerting herself, on a trying occasion, to save an injured brother from ruin, by opposing the machinations of Messrs. *Galloway*, *Wharton*, and *Towne*, has done her credit with all who know her, and entitles her to my warmest gratitude. As for my making use of the company's money, it is improbable, from Mr. *Towne's* own melancholly story; and it is a well known fact that I have been the sole support of the whole business, and that when I returned from abroad, I had money lying in merchants hands, which had been remitted by bills, for that purpose.

Left the public should be imposed upon by his seeming desirous to settle matters, I again repeat what I have a thousand times told him, that whenever he will proceed regularly and settle his accounts, and pay or give security for his debts, &c. I will cancel the contract of the company. But that is not his design. He wants to pursue the example of his patrons, to throw all the company debts, finally, upon me, by destroying the articles first. But this Mr. *Towne* need not expect. I keep 'too good a look out,' as he says, to be imposed upon, in that way, a *second time*.

The last paragraph of the piece in question, is really a *severe satire* upon Messrs. *Galloway* and *Wharton*, tho' it was designed as a panegyric on *their virtues*.

I have now done with Man *Towne*, and leave him to be dressed up for another exhibition.

It is not in the least surprizing to me that Messrs. *Galloway* and *Wharton* should think themselves capable of destroying the *Pennsylvania Chronicle*, and its publisher, when they had the vanity and presumption to undertake the oversetting the constitution of this government, and to new-model, and fill up almost every department of the state.—It has been a matter of laughter to me and others, to hear them sketch out their ambitious plans, till they worked themselves into a belief that the government would soon be in their hands—Says one, 'the reins will undoubtedly be offered to the Doctor; but I am uncertain whether he will accept them or not; but if he does not, his son will have them without scruple.' Then 'Friend *Galloway* will be Lieutenant-Governor or Chief-Justice, perhaps both.' Mr. *Wharton* was

was to be one of his Majesty's council at least—and I never heard, or read, of such a total revolution, as was to take place in all the public offices in this province. I was not entirely forgot myself, for Mr. *Wharton* whispered me in the ear—" Friend *Goddard*, if *thee will* attend to *us*, on the change, which *thee may* depend will take place, as soon as the present troubles have subsided, *thee shall* not be forgot—*Thee will* peradventure be printer to the King."——No less a man than printer to *the King's most excellent Majesty !*—He added, " WE have made *Benjamin Franklin a great man*, and it is in *our* power to make thee a great man too !—Both *Galloway* and *Wharton modestly* gave out that they were the *making* and *upholding* of Doctor *Franklin*, and that all his *philosophy* would have been of little *real* use to him, without their *countenance* and *support*. They did not absolutely promise to make me as great a *philosopher* as the Doctor, but they gave me to understand that they had all the other *necessary power* to make me a *very great man !*—But, alas ! my elevation, depended entirely on my attending to and following *their advice*. I laughed in my sleeve at this FARCE, and considered it as arising from the natural ambition and vanity of the men—a mere distempered imagination !

They frequently mentioned to certain persons in town, how much power they were possessed of.—They would boast that they could carry any points in the assembly, and that *their words* were as laws to the members, whom they could *take aside*, or *closet*, whenever they pleased. I never believed but that this was an infamous calumny ; yet I was fearful that the members might be imposed upon by the *hypocrisy* of Mr. *Wharton*, and the *artifice* of Mr. *Galloway*, as I had been, I therefore expressed my sentiments of them, with great freedom, to some warm friends of the members, who did not disagree in opinion with me.—They expressed a concern, however, that there should be any disagreement between Mr. *Galloway* and me, as they observed, he was of some use in the house as a *draftsman*, though no great genius or politician, but the other was considered a very insignificant character, as every one thinks who knows him ; and they said, as I seemed to have a *proper knowledge* of Mr. *Galloway*, " suppose you were to feed his vanity now and then by telling him that he is a better writer than Mr. *Dickinson* ; such a conduct would win his *fond heart* forever."——I could not descend to pay a servile homage at the shrine of vain-glory, pride, and self-sufficiency, I was therefore cast into the fiery furnace of Messrs. *Galloway* and *Wharton's* indignation.

I shall close this number with observing, that while Messrs. *Galloway* and *Wharton*, are permitted to have any share or influence in the legislature of this province, there will be no repose for this government ; for that ambitious principle, which formerly depopulated part of heaven, will urge them, as it has hitherto done, to sacrifice all the invaluable privileges we enjoy, to their insatiable thirst after power and place. Transported with a hurricane of zeal, (the zeal of conspirators) these plotting men, like a raging pestilence, are now meditating how to propagate their contagion, and spread a general discontent through the province, that they may rise on its ruins,

which

which is and has been their real motive, through all the *uproar* they have made, although they gild over their *poison* by specious pretence for the public welfare. To deceive the people, and accomplish their own ambitious purposes, have they not wrote, or caused to be written, panegyrics on their own *virtues*, vilified and traduced the *fairest characters* in this country, and even raked into the ashes of the dead, to find matter for *scandal*, and employment for an *envenomed pen* ?—If such men as these are countenanced by the public, we may expect to see innocent men, who should dare even *speak* against any of their iniquitous schemes, pursued with unrelenting fury, and hunted down like wild beasts of the wilderness.—Many of the friends to liberty begin to " *augur ill* " of their power—and I prophesy, unless the virtuous inhabitants stop them in their career, that they will go on in their *old business* of *sowing discord amongst brethren*, till a favourable opportunity arises, when they will immolate the liberties of their country, for their own aggrandisement, at the altar of despotism, in order to become our SOVEREIGN LORDS AND MASTERS ; from which *dishonour* and *slavery*—" GOOD LORD DELIVER US !"—

☞ To shew that Mr. Galloway's love of liberty and regard for his country, is of a piece with his justice and humanity towards me and my family, I shall publish a Postscript to this number, on Monday morning next ; containing his PATRIOTIC writings in favour of the stamp-act, with remarks on his conduct, and the reward he has met with from his country, &c. They were sent me by a friend, see No. I, page 18, that I might beware of AMERICANUS, and I think it my duty to present them to the Public for the same end.

The second edition of NUMB. I. is in the press, and will be speedily published.

Sept. 28, 1770.   WILLIAM GODDARD.

POSTSCRIPT

To Numb. II. of the

PARTNERSHIP:

OR THE

HISTORY

OF THE

RISE AND PROGRESS

OF THE

PENNSYLVANIA CHRONICLE, &c.

From the *NEW-YORK JOURNAL*, of October 30, 1766.

Mr. Holt,

THE candour and impartiality whereby you have diftinguifhed yourfelf, oblig'd you to give a place in your paper of *Auguft* the 15th, 1765, to a deteftable piece figned *Americanus*, in favour of the ftamp-act. This piece you very properly prefaced in the following manner.

"The author of the following piece is unknown to the Printer ; " *it cannot be fuppofed*, that he is an *American*, or a *friend to liberty* ; " however, he fhall not have it to fay, that he could not obtain a " fair hearing, or that his arguments were not allowed their full " weight. The caufe of liberty can receive no difadvantage from " argument and reafon : Oh! that reafon and juftice might be al- " lowed to determine the queftion !" *

Every perfon in this city who read that paper, and with whom I converfed, was of the fame opinion with you, that the piece was not written by an "*American*," or a "*friend to liberty*." It was generally fuppofed to be the production of fome native of *Great-Britain*, who had fnatched up his notions of the general interefts and of *American* rights, from the indigefted and flimfy arguments of the late arbitrary miniftry and their mercenary tools, of which arguments indeed this piece is only a collection. Not a fingle man with whom I ever fpoke on this fubject, believed that a native of *America* could be

I   fo

---

* *This preface gave Mr. Galloway great offence, infomuch that he bas had a fpleen againft the author ever fince.*

so loft to all regard for the *freedom* and *honour* of his country, as to endeavour to deftroy that facred right of taxing ourfelves, which is the fecurity of all the reft, and to fully her character with the moft bitter and fcandalous reproaches that a people can fuffer. In fhort, it could not be conceived, that an *American* could reprefent *America* as difloyal to her fovereign, *ungrateful* to her mother country, and *ftupidly* regardlefs of her own welfare; and thence infer, that the *British* parliament's taxing her was " juft," " reafonable," " neceffary," and an " *indifpenfable duty.*"

Yet this general opinion, that the above mentioned piece was not written by an *American*, was a general miftake: for by the *Philadelphia* paper of the 25th of *September* laft, I find it has been difcovered, that it was written by an *American*, by a *Pennfylvanian*, by a *lawyer*, by a *reprefentative* of the people, by a man who, as I am informed, has made a fortune by the *employments* with which his country has for fo many years intrufted him. Mr. *Jofeph Galloway*, when the fact could be no longer concealed, acknowledged by a writing under his own hand, publifhed in the paper juft mentioned, that he was the author of the piece figned " *Americanus.*"

This acknowledgment was publifhed before the late election in that province, and with an aftonifhment, which I want words to exprefs, I find in the *Philadelphia* paper of *October* the 9th,—that this affertor of *American* flavery, this reviler of *American* honour, was re-elected a *reprefentative* in affembly for the county of *Philadelphia*.

In giving fuch countenance to fuch a man, every Britifh colony receives a wound. What a blow is this to *American* freedom! to fee the people of *Pennfylvania*, hitherto diftinguifhed for their love of liberty, beftowing their favour on a man who has fo daringly attacked their deareft rights.

Mr. *Galloway*, in his acknowledgment above mentioned, infinuates, that he wrote the piece to prevent riots, and this, I am told, was the argument ufed by his friends to obtain his election. But what an *infult* is this on the underftanding of his countrymen? Could he not have fhewn the folly and wickednefs of riots, without being guilty of a greater folly and wickednefs, *in flandering his country*, and *betraying her rights?* With the fame pretence to reafon, he might beat out a man's brains, and then fay he did it to brufh off a wafp that had lighted on his head, and was going to fting him.

Pennfylvania is unhappily agitated with parties at this time, and therefore many people in that province may be willing to wink at crimes in thofe of their own fide; but certainly Mr. *Galloway* muft entertain an exceeding mean opinion of their underftanding, when he thinks that *fuch excufes* will pafs with them. When a people can be perfuaded, that liberty and flavery are the fame thing, and that there is no difference between day and night, they may perhaps alfo be perfuaded, that it is as juftifiable to flander one's country, and attack its moft valuable rights, as to argue againft riots.

I know nothing of Mr. *Galloway* but what I have feen written by him or of him in the prints, and what I have heard publicly fpoken. From hence I am convinced, that *he* had the *fame motive* to write in

favour

favour of the *ſtamp-act*, that thoſe had who were in favour of it in *Great-Britain* ; I mean, *to recommend himſelf to a domineering miniſtry*, who were reſolved on the deſtruct on of *American* liberty. My reaſons are theſe. 1. Mr. *Galloway* had the *ſame intereſt* in *England* that Mr. *Hughes* had, and as *this intereſt* had procured the office of diſtributing the ſtamps for Mr. *Hughes*, *before* he had ſignalized himſelf in the cauſe; how much *more probable* was it, that *this intereſt* would procure a *better poſt*, either of comptroller of the ſtamp-offices, or judge of one of the unconſtitutional admiralty courts for enforcing the ſtamp-act, which were very valuable offices for Mr. *Galloway*, when he had ſo *warmly exerted* himſelf in favour of this darling ſcheme ?

2dly. That Mr. *Galloway* intended to diſtinguiſh his zeal on this occaſion, is manifeſt from the pains he took to ſpread his performance throughout the continent ; by having it printed in one of our papers, and the *Philadelphia* and *Virginia* papers ; which *diligence* of his, he takes care to mention to the agent of *Pennſylvania*, in his letter dated the 20th of *September* 1765, printed in the *Philadelphia* paper of *September* the 11th, 1765.

3dly. It appears from the ſame letter that in *September* 1765, *when he wrote it, only a few days* after his *Americanus* was publiſhed here, Mr. *Galloway* thought that " Mr. *Hughes* would be able to put his commiſſion in execution in *Pennſylvania*," and commended his " *firmneſs*" for it ; ſo that he had ſome reaſon to *expect*, that his exerting himſelf in defending and enforcing the ſtamp-act, would not be *loſt labour*.

I had written thus far to you Mr. *Holt*, when the *Philadelphia* paper of laſt *Thurſday, October* 16th came to hand. You may perhaps imagine, but I cannot deſcribe to you my amazement, when I read it over and obſerved, that the man who has been publicly convicted of writing the piece ſigned " *Americanus*," was laſt *Tueſday* choſen Speaker of the aſſembly of *Pennſylvania*. I never found myſelf ſo much inclined to disbelieve my own eyes. I read the paragraph over and over; and incredible as it muſt appear to thoſe who have ſeen that piece, its author is actually promoted by the repreſentatives of a free people, to the ſeat I have mentioned !

The late ſpeaker I have heard frequently mentioned as a moderate man, of an irreproachable character, and well verſed in the buſineſs of the houſe ; but I ſuppoſe he was not violent enough for the party now prevailing there, and therefore was removed. This prevailing party, to the aſtoniſhment of every other colony that hears of their conduct, and to the grief of a great part of that province, is reſolved to change their proprietary government into a royal one, at the riſque of all thoſe envied and invaluable privileges, by which they have hitherto been ſo *eminently diſtinguiſhed* from all the reſt of the world : And every man's merit with that party, is eſtimated. as I am informed, by his ardour for, or his diſlike of that raſh project.

When I conſider this inſtance of *party fury*, my heart feels the moſt painful emotions, I ſee all diſtinctions between virtue and vice, patriotiſm and treachery, buried in blind rage : worth and moderation

tion become criminal and muſt retire ; while the deſperate party-man
ſanctifies all his actions however deteſtable, by gratifying, in a particular point, the paſſions of a people artfully inflamed by deſigning
men, who cover their own views and intereſts with ſpecious pretences
of public good.

How exactly does this conduct of the people of *Pennſylvania* juſtify
the following obſervation of the learned and ſagacious Mr. *Hume*, in
his hiſtory of *England?* " It is no wonder, (ſays he) that faction is
productive of vices of all kinds. For beſides that it inflames all the paſſions, it tends to remove thoſe great reſtraints, *honour* and *ſhame* ; when
men find *that no iniquity can loſe them the applauſe of their own party.*"

That this colony and all others to which your paper goes, may know
by this memorable example, to what exceſſes party fury may tranſport
a people, and may thereby be warned to guard againſt its fatal wild-
neſs, I beg you will reprint the piece ſigned *Americanus*, (with
the letter above referred to, a copy of which is alſo ſent to you) that
great as they will then perceive the guilt of the author to be, they
may learn that *party fury* has made him SPEAKER of the aſſembly of
Pennſylvania !

────────

Extract of a letter from Joſeph Galloway, *Eſq; dated* Philadelphia,
September 20, 1765, *to* Benjamin Franklin, *Eſq;* agent.

THE public papers will inform you of the preſent diſtracted ſtate
of the colonies, and the many *outrages and riots that have been
occaſioned by a diſlike to the ſtamp-act* ; all which have been *incited by
the principal men* of the colonies where they have been committed.
Meaſures have not been wanting to create the *ſame temper* in the people here, in which ſome have been very active. *In hopes to prevent
their ill effects,* I wrote a moderate piece, ſigned *Americanus,* publiſhed
here and at *New-York,* and ſince in *Virginia* ; wherein you will ſee
my ſentiments on the ſubject. *I am told it had a good effect in thoſe
places, as well as here, being much approved by the moderate part of the
people.* Yet we ſhould not have been free from riots here, if another
method had not been taken to prevent them. *viz.* By aſſembling
quietly, at the inſtance of Mr. *Hughes's* friends (and not by an order
from the government of the city) near 800 of the ſober inhabitants,
poſted in different parts, ready to prevent any miſchief that ſhould be
attempted by the mob, which effectually intimidated them, and kept
all tolerably quiet, only they burnt a figure they called a Stamp-Man,
and about midnight diſperſed. *Great pains have been taken to per-
ſuade and frighten Mr.* Hughes *into a reſignation of his office, but he
continues firm,* and will not reſign in any manner that ſhall do diſho-
nour to his appointment ; and, I THINK, *will be able to put his
commiſſion into execution, notwithſtanding the example ſet by other colonies.*

AT a time when *almoſt every American pen* is employed in placing
the tranſactions of the parliament of our mother country in the
moſt odious light, and in *alienating the affections* of a numerous and
loyal people *from the royal perſon* of the beſt of ſovereigns; permit
me, however unpopular the taſk, through the impartial channel of
your paper, to point out the imprudence and folly of ſuch conduct.
and

and to give a brief and true ftate of the facts included in the difpute between *Great-Britain* and her colonies. From whence the cool and unprejudiced may form a right judgment of the motives of her late conduct, and of the impropriety and rafhnefs of the method that is taken to prevail on her to alter or repeal her meafures.

It is a truth, too univerfally known, that the people of *England* are involved in a debt, under which they ftruggle with the utmoft diffi-culty. From its enormity many judicious perfons have predicted the ruin of the nation. Foreign powers rely on it, as the only founda-tion of their hopes of reducing the *Britifh* dominions. The protec-tion of *America* has, in no fmall degree, contributed to this burthen of the mother country. To the large fums of money that have been expended from the *Englifh* treafury, and the parental care of a *Britifh* parliament, we, in a great meafure, owe our prefent freedom from *Indian* barbarities, popifh cruelties and fuperftition.

The *Americans* have now acquired a confiderable fhare of proper-ty, tho' it muft be confeffed, by no means fo much as the folly and extravagance of a few, have taught our fuperiors to believe. In proportion to this property, the moft plain and evident principle of juftice, pronounces the equity of their being taxed, in order to defray the expence which their own fafety requires. If more than the colo-nies can bear, in their prefent infant ftate, is neceffary, their mother country holds herfelf ready to lend her affiftance, to fecure them from foreign invafion, oppreffion and mifery. This fhe ever has done, and as long as fhe is actuated by the principles of found policy, fhe will, and muft, continue to do.

The power of making war, of protecting and defending *Britifh* fubjects, in every part of the world, and of forming, directing and *executing that protection*, is conftitutionally vefted in the crown alone, the fubject has a right to demand it, whenever he is in danger. The right is purchafed by his allegiance, which is the reciprocal confide-ration daily paid for it. *America* confifting of a number of colonies in their infant ftate, and independent of each other, is, in a particu-lar manner, dependent on this power, and has a right to demand an exertion of it, to infure its fafety. And accordingly, during the late war, fhe received the full advantages of it, without which, in her dif-united ftate, fhe, in all probability, muft have fallen before the moft cruel and barbarous of all enemies. The prefervation of *America* is of the utmoft importance to *Great-Britain*. A lofs of it to the *Bri-tifh* crown would greatly diminifh its ftrength ; and the poffeffion of it to any other nation, would give an increafe of wealth and power totally inconfiftent with the fafety of *Britons*. If then the power of protection is rightfully and folely vefted in the crown ; if *America* is of fo much importance to her mother country ; and if it is juft and reafonable that fhe fhould contribute towards her own defence, fo ef-fential to her own and the happinefs of *Great-Britain*: *will any be fo abfurd as to deny the reafonablenefs, the neceffity, of the crown's having fome certainty that fhe will pay her proportion of aids when requifite and demanded ?*

If then it be inconteftibly juft, that *America* fhould contribute towards

wards the means of her own safety, and absolutely neceffary, that the crown, the guardian of that fafety, fhould be fupplied with the aids requifite to enable it to effect that purpofe, the next inquiry that prefents itfelf, is, *by whom is this contribution to be enforced.*

This feems to be the *grand queftion* between *Britain* and her colonies. In their prefent ftate, this can be done but by one of two modes; either *by the parliament,* or *by the feveral legiflatures of America.* The *laft method,* no doubt, would be the moft elegible and agreeable to the colonifts; and we have reafon to believe it would be alfo moft agreeable to his Majefty and his parliament, *could it with certainty and fecurity to both, be relied upon.* It can be of *little moment* to the *general welfare,* and of courfe to the King and people of *England, whether thefe aids are granted by a* Britifh *parliament, or the feveral* American *legiflatures,* provided they be really granted. Upon a difpaffionate review of the conduct of the mother country, relative to *America,* during the laft war, we fhall find it affords fufficient evidence of *this truth,* and of a tendernefs for the rights of the colonies, that ought to be retained in the moft grateful remembrance. The imminent diftrefs and danger we were in at that time, and the repeated requifitions that were tranfmitted to the crown for affiftance againft the common enemy, muft be recent in every memory. In purfuance of thefe entreaties, men and money were liberally granted by the parliament, and the wifeft plans formed by our fovereign and the miniftry for our fafety. But as *America* had life, liberty and property, to be protected, it was thought but juft, that fhe fhould alfo unite in the meafures concerted for her own prefervation. The parliament had it then, *as well as now,* in its power to compel her, without the affent of the feveral legiflatures. But inftead of making ufe of that power to levy taxes on us, the moft moderate and tender requifitions were fent over to our feveral legiflatures, requiring our proportional aids for the neceffary fervice, attended with the warmeft affurances, that a confiderable part of fuch aids fhould be repaid; thus tenderly and affectionately alluring us to the difcharge of our duty. Hence it feems manifeft, that the adminiftration would have been content with, and even preferr'd this mode, to that of having recourfe to an act of parliament, had the colonies at that time fully complied with the royal demands. Had this been done, the fufpicion would be unreafonable, that the prefent duties and impofitions would have ever been laid on in *America,* or even thought of. However, the experiment was made, but how did it prove with refpect to the intereft, the honour, and duty of *America?* Some of our legiflatures granted their proportions in time; others late, too late to be of real fervice, and fome never complied at all, though his Majefty's fubjects committed to their care, were maffacred before their eyes, and *Britifh America* was in the moft imminent danger. And it is worthy of further obfervation, that fuch was the *tendernefs* and *forbearance* of our mother country, *thus juftly provoked,* by the perverfe difobedience of fome of the colonies, at that time, when nothing lefs than the intereft and honour of the whole *Britifh* dominions were at ftake, *that they did not inftantly enforce an obedience by the method they have now taken,* which
gives

gives us so much uneasiness; but proceeding year after year, to make trial after trial, in hopes that our legislatures would comply with requisitions so reasonable and essential to our own welfare. *But all their experiments were ineffectual.* The sums of money granted by parliament for our protection, were often wasted for want of the full and timely aids of the colonies. The failure of several military expeditions were occasioned by this cause alone. And had more of the *American* provinces been equally regardless of their own immediate defence, and our mother country failed in exerting herself on the occasion, we might at this day, be the subjects of the *French* government, robbed of our liberty, and deprived of the exercise and enjoyment of our inestimable religion.

After what has been offered, *will any man of candour deny that the* Britih *government* (in whom is constitutionally vested the power of protecting us) *ought to have some security*, that sufficient aids will be granted by us, not only in any future war, but at *this time, in order to put* America *in a more defensible situation?* It is not an improbable conjecture, that in another war, she will become the scene of action, and the principal object of the contending powers. Her value and infinite importance to the possessor, justifies the thought. Should she remain in her present defenceless state, how easily would she become the prey of a foreign invader? *And how precarious her protection, should it depend on the aids to be granted by the colonies in their present disunited state, subject to the various* CAPRICES *and* HUMOURS *of our different legislatures!*

If then it be reasonable that *America* should be taxed towards her own safety, and her safety depends on her enabling the crown to secure it; if without this she may be lost to her mother country, and deprived of her civil as well as religious rights, *if she has been thus negligent of her duty, and perversely obstinate*, when those rights and her own preservation required a contrary behaviour; if she has, notwithstanding, been preserved, in a great measure, at the expence of her mother country; and, *if under her present circumstances and disunion, it appears from experience, that the crown can have no dependance* that she will act differently on future occasions; does it not then become *the indispensable duty of a* Britih *parliament to interfere, and compel her to do* what is reasonable and necessary for *her preservation!* Shall the colonies be lost to the *Britih* dominions thro' their own obstinacy, caprice and *folly*; and shall not *Great-Britain*, whose interest is inseparably united with theirs, *endeavour to prevent it?* Shall she stand by, an inactive spectator, indifferent to her own and their welfare, and not make the *least essay* towards avoiding the consequential mischief?

The highest degree of vanity certainly cannot prompt us to imagine that our sovereign and his parliament will be *intimidated* by the *irreverent censures*, and *disloyal menaces* of the *Americans, in their present disunited and defenceless condition.* It is a proof of the greatest infatuation to conceive, that we can *bully* the *Britih* nation, now at peace with the whole world, and possessed of strength which the united powers of *France* and *Spain* could not subdue. Let us then con-
vert

vert our idle threats into dutiful remonstrances. Reveal to them the poverty of our circumstances, and rectify the false representations which they have received of our wealth. Show them our incapacity to pay the impositions which they have laid upon us, without more freedom of commerce, and a circulating medium to carry on that commerce. Tell them, that should they make a thousand acts of parliament to oblige us, we cannot give what we have not, and what they prevent us from procuring for want of due attention to our circumstances. And tell them our incapacity to pay the debt already due to the *British* merchants; our inability to take off their future manufactures, and the impossibility of our contributing to the wealth, power and glory of our mother country; unless she will relax her present measures, which so essentially affect her own as well as our welfare.

And as we claim the right of laying and levying our own taxes, by our own representatives, let us point out some rational method, which will afford a confident dependance to the crown, that this shall be done whenever necessary for the safety of our country.——If an united legislature of the colonies, free from the objections arising from the present state of our distinct and several legislatures, is what we aim at, let us form some rational plan of such a legislature, and lay it before the sovereign and the parliament, or prevail on our several assemblies, to execute the plan by their several acts of assembly. Or if we prefer a common legislature with our mother country, *petition for the right of sending members to parliament*. Upon the whole, let us convince our mother country, that the colonies will, at all times, grant such reasonable aids, as shall be necessary for our own preservation, whenever it becomes the duty of the crown to require them; for without this, it will be difficult, if not impossible, to persuade her, that the law of necessity, *which is superior to all laws, will not justify the imposition of taxes without our assent,* for so necessary a purpose.

It is with pleasure I hear, the colony of *Massachusetts* has taken the lead in this important measure. A general invitation from the assembly of that colony has been lately sent to the several houses of representatives of the *American* provinces, requesting a meeting of a committee from each, to take under their consideration the late stamp-act, &c. and thereupon to form a general and united dutiful and loyal representation of the true circumstances of *American* affairs, to their sovereign and the parliament. Under a confidence, no doubt, that they will be able to convince them, that the true interest of *America*, is the real interest of *Great-Britain*, and that they shall succeed in obtaining relief from whatever is grievous and oppressive to the colonies.

While these wise and prudent measures are prosecuting by the several assemblies of the people, it is to be hoped, that those indecent reflections which have already been too often repeated in our public papers, will be no longer continued, as they only tend to create in the minds of the weak and ignorant, a spirit of disloyalty against the crown, and hatred against the people of *England*; and to excite the resentment of our superiours against the *Americans*, and thereby involve them into difficulties more burthensome and inconvenient, than those we now so loudly complain of.   AMERICANUS.

ADVERTISEMENT.

I Have the fatisfaction to acquaint the Public, that on the firft inft. (the anniverfary
election in this province) a great number of the
Freeholders and Freemen of this city and county,
from a conviction of the impropriety of com-
mitting the guardianfhip of their facred rights to
a man of Mr. *Galloway's* principles, one who
has not only been guilty of flagrant acts of injuftice and inhumanity towards individuals, but
bafely proftituted his pen to enflave and ruin his
native country, at the moft critical and important period known in the annals of *America,*
nobly difdained to give him their fuffrages, with
a firmnefs and independance of fpirit that reflects unfading luftre on their characters.—Such
a conduct was perfectly confiftent--for it would be
prepofterous to fuppofe, that a man without *virtue* in his *heart,* could be a proper *reprefentative*
of a *virtuous people.*—Alarmed at the refolution
and zeal of the electors here, Mr. *Galloway,*
with a meannefs of fpirit that wants a name, fled
to *Bucks* County, and, by artifice, *obtruded* himfelf upon that county as a reprefentative, before
the electors there could be fully advifed of the
caufe and manner of his precipitate flight from this
city.—They are now better informed—and it
is not doubted but they will embrace the firft
opportunity to convince the world, that they are
actuated by the fame love of juftice, and regard
for the liberties of their country, as their brethren of this city and county.

WILLIAM GODDARD.

Philadelphia, October 8, 1770.

AN ADDRESS

Lately prefented to

J---- G------- Efq.

Sir,

⟨decorative border with W⟩ E whofe names are underwritten, citizens of *Philadel-phia*, beg leave to return you our hearty thanks for publifhing the piece called " The Speech &c."

THIS performance with Mr. *Dickinfon's* Reply to it, have afforded fuch infinite *laughter* and *delight* to us and many other of his majefty's liege fubjects, that we earneftly requeft you will be pleafed, as foon as poffible, to publifh another treatife, as we do not doubt from the experience we have had of your writing, that any thing coming from your pen, muft give us the higheft *entertainment.*

SINCERELY wifhing in your own emphatic expreffions, that your " powers of *life*, and *vital* motion" may be preferved for our *exceeding great mirth* and *recreation*, and that it may be long before " the *midnight gloom* and *fatal death* put an end to your ftruggles.".

We are your *truly obliged*

Humble fervants,

T----W-----	J-----N-----	S-----I------	W-----I-----˙
J------W-----	J-----W----	C-----L----	A-----D-----
P-----B-----	G----C-----	A----.L----	J------I------